Telling Stories Your Way

Storytelling and reading aloud
in the classroom

Bob Barton

Pembroke Publishers Limited

43282291   6/03

For Kim, Doug, Michelle and Philip
— good listeners all

©2000 **Pembroke Publishers**
538 Hood Road
Markham, Ontario, Canada L3R 3K9
www.pembrokepublishers.com

Distributed in the U.S. by Stenhouse Publishers
P.O. Box 360
York, Maine 03909
www.stenhouse.com

We acknowledge the financial support of the Government of Canada through
the Book Publishing Industry Development Program (BPIDP) for our publishing activities.

Canadian Cataloguing in Publication Data

Barton, Robert
   Telling stories your way: storytelling and reading aloud in the classroom

ISBN 1-55138-119-2

1. Storytelling. 2. Oral reading. I. Title.

LB1042.B374 2000   372.67'7   C99-932851-4

Editor: Kate Revington
Cover Design: John Zehethofer
Cover Photography: Ajay Photographics
Typesetting: Jay Tee Graphics Ltd.

Printed and bound in Canada
0 9 8 7 6 5 4 3 2 1

Contents

Introduction

An article I read not long ago in the *New York Times* described the growing popularity of storytelling as entertainment for adults in bars and clubs across the United States: "The evenings draw on the traditions of professional yarnspinners who tend to tell and retell the same stories, often fable-like in tone. In the past such tellers were hired by schools to recount stories to pupils. Now they find themselves in cafes and bars, regaling adults." (May 1999)

The writer cited numerous possible reasons for this renewed interest in storytelling, including the level of interaction with the audience. Storytelling among adults can be "a vital way to establish community in the sterile environment of the electronic age."

Some years ago when I was teaching at the Ontario Teacher Education College, it became part of my practice to begin each class with a story. Initially, I was a bit nervous. After all, my students were adults. I quickly learned, however, that if I omitted the story at the beginning of a class there was much disappointment. I continue to meet some of my former students in their schools and it's the stories they remember. Many make a point of telling me that reading aloud and storytelling is a priority in their classrooms.

I don't know why I was hesitant to tell stories to my adult students. After all, storytelling, the most ancient of art forms, was the chief entertainment of rulers, warriors, aristocrats, and peasants across centuries. Its current popularity is part of a continuum that reaches back to the beginnings of humankind.

The current renewed interest referred to in the *Times* piece can probably be traced to the strong revival of storytelling in the United States during the 1970s. There are some community storytelling associations (eg., The Detroit Storytelling League) with roots stretching back to the turn of the century; however, it was the establishment of an annual storytelling festival in Jonesborough, Tennessee, by the National Association for the Perpetuation and Preservation of Storytelling (NAPPS), now The National Storytelling Association, which brought tremendous attention to storytelling and continues to do so.

In Canada, around the same time, the Storytellers School of Toronto played a significant part in developing, in altogether different fashion from the NAPPS, a strong and committed storytelling community that helped to rekindle interest across the country.

In both places, storytelling was happening in the adult community more than anywhere else.

During the twentieth century, storytelling's perceived educational value has waxed and waned.

Early in the century it waxed due to the efforts of adherents to the Froebel philosophy. This philosophy recognizes the human need for story, something that allows children to reflect on their own experiences and that provides a source of rich vicarious experience.

After this impetus to storytelling in schools faded, Gordon Wells's Bristol study in the 1970s aroused interest in the education community. Wells's study highlighted the importance of story in children's literacy development. The combination of new research findings and the increased availability of professional storytellers willing to work in schools caused many educators to look again at the value of storytelling.

During the 1980s academics and scholars such as Shirley Brice Heath (*Ways with Words*) and Carol Fox (*At the Very Edge of the Forest*) made more contributions to the literature on the role of story in children's lives. Fox, in particular, presented a very powerful analysis on the primacy of narrative in the development of children's imaginative, cognitive, and linguistic competence. Educators such as Vivian Gussin Paley in the United States (*The Boy Who Would Be a Helicopter: The Uses of Storytelling in the Classroom* and *The Girl with the Brown Crayon: How Children Use Stories to Shape Their Lives*) and Betty Rosen in England (*And None of It Was Nonsense*) also made significant contributions to an understanding of storytelling's importance in the classroom.

Education initiatives such as The National Oracy Project in England and the Peel Talk Project in Canada served to highlight the importance of oral narrative in the talk continuum, as well.

However, issues other than storytelling have caught the attention of educators and parents. More prescriptive curricula, greater demands for accountability, and enormous demographic changes in the teaching profession are consuming tremendous time and effort. Interest in storytelling now seems to be on the decline.

I remain convinced though that many teachers value the art and with a little encouragement will want to develop the knack for storytelling. In her book *Shapers and Polishers*, Betty Rosen argues that if narrative is a powerful force, a liberating activity, a giver of articulateness and worth to students, why shouldn't it be for teachers?

> Few teachers of language actually write . . . or even consciously talk
> . . . creatively in the way they expect their students to do. Thus we
> neither develop our own language as we could nor surprise ourselves
> by our own skills in manipulating words to creative ends.

Storytelling can put this situation to rights.

We are all born storytellers. Each and everyone of us tells stories of our own life experiences daily. When we are telling the stories of our lives, we muster the deepest feelings and the most interesting details we can to grip our listeners. Those skills that we use in such a natural way are the very ones required to get the stories onto our tongues.

If this book has one central message, it is this: a willingness to explore and experiment is one of the greatest assets you can bring to storytelling or reading aloud. In the pages that follow you will learn some easy and effective ways to know and tell a story. Developing your own method and style is important. There is no intention here of locking you into a pattern.

Many people are concerned about remembering a story or getting it right — this needn't become an obstacle. The techniques outlined in the text will help you to deal with this.

If you are worried about being self-conscious in front of a group, don't be. When a story is told so much is happening. For one thing, you reveal much about yourself as a person. Listeners sense this quickly. They appreciate your desire to reach out and make contact with them. Stories are wonderful meeting places. As author Janet Lunn puts it, "The whole world is one great conversation, which is carried out through telling stories and it is this great conversation that holds us together."

If there is any difficulty to overcome it will probably be how to find a story you want to tell. I have made many suggestions throughout the book to help you get started.

For parents who wish to help make stories and reading a part of their children's lives, providing shared experiences with stories is essential. Especially for older children who are reading independently, reading aloud and telling stories together is the best way I know to keep the desire to read alive.

First and foremost, I believe stories are for pleasure. A sixth grade girl wrote this comment to me after a storytelling session in her school: "I'm writing a story called The Quest. Sometimes I feel like stopping and not doing any more, but when you came it inspired me and I kept on going." I believe that student was re-energized by the stories that day in a way that only she could know. Her mind, her spirit, her imagination had been touched and her insightful comment revealed that pleasure had rekindled her enthusiasm. Although I never spoke to her in person she signed her letter, "Your greatest fan."

And that suggests another reason I value storytelling. It is a powerful way of creating a happy person-to-person relationship even among a room full of strangers.

ONE

Edging into Storytelling

"I knew a sailor once," said Miss Éclair, gazing toward the window.
The other two ladies looked at Miss Éclair with a curiosity that had not been freshened for many years.
Unclasping her hands and laying them palms down on the table, Miss Éclair gazed through a mist of time as she moved one index finger to touch the other. She said again, this time with a voice full of resignation and longing:
"I knew a sailor once."

From *Amy's Eyes* by Richard Kennedy

For many years, people have approached me after a storytelling session and confessed that although they enjoy listening to stories, they doubt they could get up in front of a group and tell one. Some people have admitted that they lack enough courage to read aloud. Many others I have met are interested in and enthusiastic about sharing stories out loud, but aren't certain how to go about it. These experiences have prompted me to offer some practical advice and suggestions on ways to get started.

We are all natural storytellers. Everything that happens to us in our lives is filed at the back of our minds in containers called stories.

Can you imagine a society where stories are not told? Author Monica Hughes paints such a picture in *Beyond the Dark River*.

"Who is your chronicler? Let me talk to her . . . to him."
At the blank looks Daughter-of-She-Who-Came-After stamped her foot. "Who is the one who makes the songs of your tribe's history and teaches the rest? Who remembers who was born in which moon of

what year . . . who can tell the weather and what the harvest was like. Do not pretend to be stupid. You must tell me."

Benjamin shook his head. "We have no chronicler. The births and deaths are written in the Leut record, which the Preacher keeps. But we have no songs."

"Our only songs are the ones whereby we praise God," the Preacher snapped. "All else is vanity."

Daughter-of-She-Who-Came-After stared. "How can you be a tribe if you have no memory of who you are, or who your fathers and mothers were back to the beginning? If you cannot remember who it was who killed the great bear in the winter of little snow? If you cannot tell ahead in which years it will rain all through the summer because it has always done so in that kind of year? You are a people at the mercy of the moment if you do not reverence the past."

To be "at the mercy of the moment" is a terribly lonely prospect. What a strange world it would be without stories! Often in a workshop young and old alike will say: "Oh, I don't know any stories. Nothing exciting ever happens to me." But we *do* have stories. They may be ones we heard as children, they may be ones we tell about our lives — they're there alright.

Building Your Personal World

P. L. Travers, author of *Mary Poppins,* recognizes the importance of stories. A few years ago, she wrote an article in the *New York Times* entitled "Adventures into Childhood." Travers told a story about three brothers who were new to her neighborhood. The boys had tried to stinkbomb her mailbox and were caught in the act. In conversation afterwards with their father, Travers said of the boys, "It's just that they don't know where they are. They're lonely. They have no sense of place." She urged the father to spend more time with his sons and to help them develop a sense of place, or locality. Make up stories about local shopkeepers, a hole in the road, works of public art, she pleaded. "This way you build your personal world like a bird building a nest. A straw here, a memory there." For Travers, the possibilities for creating and telling stories were infinite.

Travers's advice remains fixed in my memory. What a wonderful, practical idea for parents and teachers — get involved with your children through your own stories!

When I meet people interested in learning about storytelling, personal stories are often the first we share. Many of these are *home stories,* which normally don't have much appeal beyond the intimacy of the family, but do trigger remembrances in others and release a stream of memories.

Nicholas Tucker, who teaches developmental psychology at the University of Sussex, observes that these home stories serve many important functions. He agrees with P. L. Travers that such stories enable us to develop a strong sense of home, of neighborhood, and of community. He also points out that the child is often the centre of these tales, appearing as the hero or heroine. The immediacy of such stories connects powerfully with the child and may even assist the child to overcome fears and anxieties.

Home stories can enable children to learn about a time in their lives that they were too young to remember. In our home, my wife engaged in this kind of storytelling. Our children were not the centre of amazing fantasies, but they were the featured characters of simple home adventures. To this day, my now grownup children still request those stories: "Tell me about the time when I was three years old and drove our neighbor's car down Chedoke Avenue while she was carrying groceries into the house."

Traditional lore is also part of home stories. Some of it survives in the form of rhymes, chants, songs, superstitions, or sayings. I seldom meet a person who can't remember some "little lesson of life" heard while growing up.

What I love about these family sayings is how much is implied about a family's moral code in such condensed and forcible language. Here's a sampling I've collected on my travels.

- The trouble with the devil is he plays good tunes. (Northern Ireland)
- Judge not your friends by outward show. For feathers float and pearls lie low. (Nova Scotia)
- Lie with dogs and you rise with fleas. (Jamaica)
- You can't teach what you don't know anymore than you can come back from where you haven't been. (Nebraska)

- About ketchup: You shake and shake and shake the bottle. None'll come and then a lot'll. (Australia)

The impact of this kind of home story is beautifully documented in Alice Kane's *Songs and Sayings of an Ulster Childhood* where "everything was an occasion for a verse a song or a wild cry of delight or protest." All of the rhymes, songs, sayings, and chants in the book are set within a context of family and community, thus heightening the impact of the material.

> My first real memories are of Mother, whom we called Mummy, mostly shadowy ones and mostly having to do with getting bathed or dressed. A very clear picture is the one of being lifted out of a bath, wrapped in a large towel which covered me from head to foot and being rubbed vigorously to a cry of "Where's the baby? Where's the baby? Oh, there she is!"
>
> After the towelling my feet were dried carefully to the rhyme:
> This little piggy went to market
> This little piggy stayed at home
> This little piggy had bread and butter
> But this little piggy had none
> And this little piggy cried "Wee wee wee
> All the way home."

Discovering the Universality of Nursery Rhymes

As a young teacher with little time to learn a folk or a fairy tale after lesson preparation, nursery rhymes became a mainstay of my storytelling repertoire. At first I looked for pieces rich in sound and with strong, driving rhythms that the students and I could chant together.

> One-ery, two-ery, ziccary, zan;
> Hollow bone, crackabone ninery ten:
> Spittery spot, it must be done;
> Twiddleum, twaddleum Twenty one.

The more I searched the nursery rhyme collections, the more fascinated I became with their forceful, direct language. For example:

Cross-patch,
Draw the latch
Sit by the fire and spin;
Take a cup
And drink it up,
Then call your neighbors in.

And this one:

Where have you been today, Billy, my son?
Where have you been today, my only man?
I've been a wooing, mother, make my bed soon,
For I'm sick at heart, and fain would lay down.

What have you ate today, Billy, my son?
What have you ate today, my only man?
I've ate eel-pie, mother, make my bed soon,
For I'm sick at heart, and shall die before noon.

In these powerful nursery rhymes, there lurked resonances of legends, myths, hero tales, and ballads. For example, "Where have you been today, Billy, my son?" echoes the ballad *Lord Randal* in just eight lines.

I began to pay close attention to these stories and to search for connections. Far from being pure nonsense, these rhymes turned out to have intricate family trees and relatives all over the world. Here's one I followed:

On Saturday night I lost my wife
And where do you think I found her?
Up in the moon, singing a tune
With all the stars around her.

This short rhyme raised many questions.

How strange, this woman's exit into space! Had she gone willingly? What did her singing have to do with the incident? Did anyone try to go after her? How did she adapt to a new environment? Was she able to return? What would she miss from her earthly home?

My quest for answers to these questions yielded myths and folktales too numerous to catalogue completely: "The Star Maiden," which appears in Virginia Haviland's *North American Legends*; "The Star

Brides" (pages 114–16, chapter 7); "Daughter of the Moon, Son of the Sun," as retold by James Riordan in *The Sun Maiden and the Crescent Moon: Siberian Folktales*; and "The Moon Maidens," a Chinese tale in Shirley Climo's *A Pride of Princesses*.

I also noted several types of nursery rhymes. The familiar "Ring a ring o' roses, a pocket full of posies" sat cheek-by-jowl with this bizarre verse:

> There was an old woman, her name it was Peg;
> Her head was of wood and she wore a cork leg
> The neighbors all pitched her into the water,
> Her leg was drowned first, and her head followed after.

There were well-developed sagas such as the ones that Maurice Sendak illustrated in *Hector Protector* and *As I Went Over the Water*,

> Hector Protector was dressed all in green.
> Hector Protector was sent to the queen.
> The queen did not like him; no more did the king.
> So Hector Protector was sent home again.

tall tales, for example, about a Derby Ram whose wool

> Reached up into the sky
> The eagles build their nests there
> For I heard the young ones cry.

and short stories such as the one about the old woman whose pig refused to jump over the stile.

Easing into Storytelling

Structure in the nursery rhyme literature also caught my interest.

> Old woman, old woman
> Shall we go a'shearing?
>
> Speak a little louder, sir,
> I'm very thick of hearing.
>
> Old woman, old woman
> Wilt thee go a'gleanin?

Speak a little louder, sir,
I cannot tell the meanin.

Old woman, old woman,
Wilt thee go awalkin?

Speak a little louder, sir,
Or what's the use of 'talkin'.

Old woman, old woman,
Shall I come and kiss thee?

I think I hear some better, sir,
The Lord in Heaven bless ye.

The question and answer format of selections such as "Old woman, old woman" was everywhere — folk songs, poetry, short stories, playground lore.

Old buzzard, old buzzard
What are you doing?
Picking up sticks.
What are you doing that for?
To build a fire.
Why do you need a fire?
To roast a chick.
Where will you get it?
Out of your flock!

The question/answer structure quickly became one my students explored as a container for their own stories. Such stories also made interesting tandem performance pieces with one individual or group handling the questions; the other, the answers.

Burnie's Hill

What's in there?
Gold and money.
Where's my share?
The mousie's run away with it.
Where's the mousie?
In her housie.

Where's the housie?
In the woods.
Where's the woods?
The fire burnt it.
Where's the fire?
The water quenched it.
Where's the water?
The brown bull drank it.
Where's the brown bull?
Back o' Burnie's Hill.

Where's Burnie's Hill?
All clad in snow.
Where's the snow?
The sun melted it.
Where's the sun?
High, high in the sky.

Infinity stories also became a class favorite. We made a game of it; I would tell an infinity story and as soon as the students figured out how the story was working, they would chime in. The fun was to be the first one to chime in and to have guessed the pattern correctly. Here are two common examples:

It was a dark and stormy night
And I was standing on the deck
And the captain said to me,
"Tell me a story my boy!"
So I began.
It was a dark and stormy night, *etc.*

The boy octopus said to the girl octopus
"Want to walk along the beach
hand in hand, hand in hand, hand in hand, *etc.*

But the favorite was always

Pete and Repete sat on a fence
Pete fell off
Who was left?
Repete!

Pete and Repete sat on a fence . . .

Infinity stories led us to cumulative stories ("This is the house that Jack built") and chronological stories ("Solomon Gundy"), as well as to rhyme rhythm patterns ("I had a cat and the cat pleased me, I fed my cat by yonder tree; Cat goes fiddle-i-fee"). All of these patterns were borrowed by the children in their own story writing.

In the process of exploring these stories the students and I were growing in our expressiveness and our willingness to experiment with our voices. Before long we were playing with words, trying on roles, and discovering new ways to release print from the pages of books.

My students began to make connections with their own living oral traditions and were soon swapping sayings and riddles with me.

What's green and comes out at night?
(A vampickle.)

Little did they know that they were educating me. They weren't familiar with many nursery rhymes and some had only recently become acquainted with the "three threes" — "Three Bears," "Three Pigs," and "Three Billy Goats Gruff" — but they had their own stories in the form of wordplay and schoolyard chants and they told them with incredible skill. They also took great pride in teaching me. If only I had had the foresight then to record what they recited. Years later when I read Iona and Peter Opie's *The Lore and Language of School-children,* I realized the opportunities I had missed.

As I look back forty years, I realize how effortlessly I had eased into storytelling. The oral tradition with its built-in tricks (rhyme, rhythm, repetition) had done for me what it had done for all human beings since the dawn of storytelling — helped me to remember.

🍎 TWO

Don't Tell Us Any of Those "Once Upon a Time Stories"

*We all tell stories, but ours are mostly about what's happened to us or
what we think has happened to us. Stanley's are weird. He tells stories
about how when the sun goes down at night it turns into a golden fish
and swims about and that's why you must never go into the water at
night or you might make it angry and it won't come up again in the
morning. He tells stories about how the stars sing and how you can catch
the wind if you run fast enough and he says there are animals who live
in the clouds. Look, he says you can see the shapes of them. Freda says,
"That's not true, Stanley. You're only making that up, aren't you?"*

From *The Voyage of QV66*, by Penelope Lively

The unruly band of nine-year-olds burst into the library, galumphed
across the room, and threw themselves down on the carpet at my feet.

"Watcha gonna do with us, mister?" they asked.

"I've come to tell you a story," I replied. There was an immediate
wrinkling of noses and screwing up of faces, accompanied by a chorus
of groans. "Don't you like stories?" I asked.

"Don't tell us any of those 'Once Upon a Time Stories,' " ordered a
girl close to my knees.

"What's a Once Upon a Time Story?" I asked innocently.

"You know," they all snorted, "those fairy stories."

"What would you like instead?" I asked.

"We want action!" they demanded.

I immediately launched into a fairytale, carefully omitting the

18

"Once Upon a Time" opening. At the conclusion of the story, there was much nodding of heads and all-around agreement that the story had been rather good.

"Do you know," said the outspoken young lady beside my knees, "that's just like the soaps on TV."

Her observation was accurate. That fairytale was indeed the stuff of melodrama. It was more however. It was also a powerful imaginative experience and those difficult-to-reach children had been swept along by it.

But the children made an important point: they wanted a story with action. When choosing a story to share aloud this criterion is important.

How to Select a Story

Giving advice about story selection is tricky. We aren't all interested in the same stories. Stories are a very personal matter.

You will find yourself sifting through dozens of stories in order to find one that appeals to you. Don't be discouraged. Just when you think you'll never find a story you like, up it pops. I spend hours and hours poring over anthologies and most of what I have learned and continue to learn is by trial and error. It is in the telling of the story that so much about the tale is discovered. Often I will tell a story a few times and then drop it. What I thought I liked about the material when I first found it has not worked out.

You must like a story to tell it successfully. Your confidence in it goes a long way toward helping you put it across sincerely. The story should also have some quality that makes it worth sharing. What truths, images, discoveries does it contain? How does it help us to understand humanity? In his *Read-Aloud Handbook* Jim Trelease says, "More than helping them to read better, more than exposing them to good writing, more than developing their imaginations, when we read aloud to children we are helping them to find themselves and to discover some meaning in the scheme of things."

I learned quickly that a good story is a good story for everyone; even young children can understand much more when listening than they can when reading for themselves. For several summers, I was a storyteller-in-residence at Artpark in Lewiston, New York. I was faced with an interesting selection problem. The majority of audiences that came to the storytelling theatre were composed of adults, yet at any given moment the audience might contain preschoolers, children from a local day camp or teenagers. Working with varied audiences and paying attention to what worked and what didn't helped me to develop some guidelines for story selection.

The chart on the next page shows what a storyteller might keep in mind when matching stories and audiences.

Here are brief descriptions of some stories that have wide-ranging appeal.

A fast-paced amusing story works well with both a young audience or a family audience comprised of babes in arms to seniors. One I particularly like is *The Little Old Lady Who Was Not Afraid of Anything*.

The folk roots of this picture book by Linda Williams are found in *English Fairy Tales*, collected by Joseph Jacobs. There the story is called "The Strange Visitor."

> A woman was sitting at her reel one night;
> And still she sat, and still she reeled, and still
>   she wished for company.
>
> In came a pair of broad broad soles, and sat down
>   at the fireside;
> And still she sat, and still she reeled, and still
>   she wished for company.
>
>   . . .

Gradually, bit by bit legs attach themselves to the soles, knees perch on legs, and thighs rise above knees until the woman is confronted by some sort of spectre.

Williams assembles her story in similar fashion, beginning with the lady meeting a pair of shoes in the woods, followed by baggy trousers and so on. It may sound scary but it's not. The story is clever and funny and invites audience participation. The author adds a very satisfying ending which provides a win-win situation for the story characters and for us, the audience, too.

If I had to choose a story that has *everything* my nod would go to "Owl," a wonderful Haitian folktale in Diane Wolkstein's *The Magic Orange Tree*. From its arresting opening line, "Owl thought he was ugly," to an ending which produces shock, laughter, and hushed

Finding the Right Match between Audience and Story

Audience	Characteristics of Stories	Examples
Preschool to early primary	stories featuring action, repetition, and ordinary situations which contain elements of the extraordinary or the mysterious	"The Story of the Turnip," in *Russian Fairy Tales* collected by Aleksandr Afanas'ev "Tipingee," in *The Magic Orange Tree* by Diane Wolkstein "The Half Chick," in *Best Loved Folktales of the World* by Joanna Cole "The One Turnip Garden," in *Ten Small Tales* by Celia Lottridge I especially like the stories of Richard Hughes from *The Wonder Dog* with this age group.
Junior and middle school	stories featuring action, powerful characters, and the elements of surprise, humor or some bizarreness	"Jorinda and Joringel" (Grimm Brothers) *The Boy Who Drew Cats* (Japanese — Lafcadio Hearn as reteller) "There's One Day for the Victim," in *Bury My Bones But Keep My Words* by Tony Fairman Richard Kennedy's "Come Again in the Spring," in *Richard Kennedy: Collected Stories*, is an excellent example.
Young adult/ adult/family	stories featuring action; elements of surprise, humor, and suspense; believable, interesting characters; and powerful introductions	"Fair, Brown and Trembling," in *Irish Folk Tales* edited by Henry Glassie "Lanval," in *Proud Knight, Fair Lady: The Twelve Lais of Marie de France* translated by Naomi Lewis *How They Broke Away to Go to the Rootabaga Country*, by Carl Sandburg The literary tales of Hans Christian Andersen and Oscar Wilde are excellent examples.

stillness, the story grabs you and doesn't let go. It zeroes in on extreme differences and how those differences can mar the life of an individual. Owl's incredible lack of self-confidence is made even more painful by the presence of his cocksure cousin, Rooster. The song and dance sequences in the story provide a glorious opportunity for audience involvement and bring some comic relief to the growing tension.

Another story with wide-ranging appeal is "Cap O Rushes." There are many variants of it available but I particularly like the version in Joseph Jacobs's *English Fairy Tales*. "Cap O Rushes" is a wonderful story to tell and works well for all ages.

A young woman of privilege falls victim to her father's misunderstanding of her feelings toward him. Exiled, she must go out into the world with nothing. She's made of the right stuff, however. Not only does she take charge of her life cleverly and skillfully she also engineers a reconciliation with her father. The story line is lean and spare, easy to learn, and a delight to tell. Its Cinderella-like resemblance involves listeners quickly.

Highly suspenseful stories that hook listeners immediately work best with groups of young adolescents. Initially, these young people are often reluctant to show any signs of interest or responsiveness, the result, I think, of little exposure to oral storytelling. They may think the whole experience somewhat beneath them. Grabbing their attention through a powerful introduction helps.

Undoubtedly, one of the best examples of a suspenseful tale is Richard Kennedy's *Come Again in the Spring*. In this gripping drama, a feisty old man named Hark finds himself caught up in a life-and-death battle of wits with the Grim Reaper. The plot is fast-paced and episodic and the outcome is in doubt right up to the last few lines. A cliffhanger, it provides a very satisfying experience. I never tire of telling this story.

Whenever storytelling is described, the word *spell* is often used. A story that really does cast a spell is the wonderful modern fairytale, *The Spider's Palace* by Richard Hughes. I first thought this a good story for younger children, but I have been pleasantly surprised to discover that teenagers and adults are even more intrigued by it.

The Spider's Palace is set in a tangly, snake-infested forest with a girl poised "on the edge of the twigs where even the snakes were too terrified to come after her," ready for her ascent into the clouds on the back of a spider. Magic is everywhere. Anything can happen and it does.

The subject matter is compelling, the situation is serious, and the matter-of-fact tone of the language holds everyone in thrall. Truly it is an extraordinary story.

One ten-year-old girl had this comment to make about it: "I am crazy to know what happened to the girl after she saw the spider turn into a man. Will they live happily ever after? I like those stories a lot, they make you have to imagine what would happen next."

What further endorsement could I offer?

From a little-known, but newly reprinted, collection of four stories by Russell Hoban, "La Corona and the Tin Frog" works beautifully out loud. The tiny title story, exacting in detail, yet large in possibilities, is about a love affair between a wind-up frog and the beautiful lady found on the label inside the lid of a cigar box. The romance takes place entirely inside the box with a supporting cast that includes a magnifying glass, a seashell, and a yellow, cloth measuring-tape. Hoban has created a fascinating world that intrigues and entertains.

Other noteworthy characteristics of good stories for the telling are their length (mostly short), their structure (recurring action or repetition), and their simple, direct language. Interesting words and expressions, little chants, and turns of phrase all matter and for the most part stories such as I've just noted possess an oral style.

You will find that many of the folktales you read these days have been beautifully written by a reteller and resemble the literary short story. The words look terrific to the eye but will need to be reworked to appeal to the ear.

Compare the following introductions to the same story, "Soap, Soap, Soap." The first, from Richard Chase's *Grandfather Tales*, works well orally; the second, retold in *Tales, Myths and Legends* edited by Pie Corbett, bears a greater resemblance to the literary short story.

> One time there was a woman fixin' to wash clothes and she found out she didn't have no soap, so she hollered to her little boy and told him to go to the store for soap, says "Don't you forget now — soap."

> A long time ago before the days of electricity, there were no such things as washing machines, so people in the countryside had to go down to the river to do their washing.
>
> Bad weather could be a problem, of course, and so it was for Jack's mother, for it had been raining non-stop for weeks and she now had a

great pile of dirty sheets and clothing. Well, at last one day the sun came out and she was really pleased. Quickly she got the dirty washing down to the river and dumped it all into the water — and only at that point did she realize that she hadn't got any soap. She didn't want to leave all her wet washing there and now it was too heavy to carry back to the house. She needed help, but the only person around was her son, Jack. Now she loved him and he loved her, but the problem was he was so forgetful.

Reworking isn't difficult to do. Think about the natural rhythms of the spoken word. Get the story into your own words, plain, concrete words that appeal to the senses, and tell it, tell it, tell it — in your head, to the mirror, to the wall, to a willing listener. Doing this will free the story considerably. Just seeing that other versions of a story exist will liberate you from the written text.

Stories live through their characters. When Old Hark, Owl, La Corona, and Cap O Rushes enter our lives, they are not forgotten quickly. That is why a keen awareness of character helps greatly when choosing stories.

Listening to others read and tell stories effectively guides story selection. Many a time I have passed over a story only to hear someone else tell it and realize, through another's viewpoint, aspects of the story I had never considered. For this reason, I have never been too concerned if the story I tell is one with which the listeners are familiar.

Author and poet Kevin Crossley-Holland says that "the storyteller is a window through which the story must shine." When you tell a story, you are the go-between who has carefully worked with the story and who imparts nuances and innuendoes with your voice, gestures, and facial expressions. Each time a story is told, it is born again for the listeners and for the storyteller.

Working with Traditional Tales

There are thousands of stories from which to make your choices, but you cannot go wrong with folktales. The familiar story patterns, spare colorful language, compelling characters, and wide-ranging subject matter all contribute to their wide appeal.

Molly Bang's retelling of an Indian folktale, *The Old Woman and the*

Rice Thief, is a good example. In this rollicking romp, an old woman who has been robbed repeatedly of her "cold boiled rice and her warm puffed rice" decides to take matters into her own hands and complain to the local Rajah. Along the road to the Rajah's palace she meets a scorpion fish, a wood apple, a cow pat, a razor blade, and a crocodile, who all offer assistance. The old woman turns them down at first, but is later forced to relent. The results are explosive.

Even the youngest listener can figure out how the story, with its cumulative and repetitive structure, is working and begin to predict what will happen next. At the same time, the audience can take part in the story. Sometimes I say: "Now that you know how the story works, I'll be the old woman; you be the razor blade. Who speaks now?" Such an opportunity to join in makes this story much fun for both the storyteller and the listeners.

This story is known as a *formula tale*. Generally, such tales have a quite simple structure, yet they contain some of the best qualities not only of folktales, but of storytelling. They are action-packed and the repetition and refrains propel them along briskly.

Traditional tales have much to teach about language. The story patterns offer children an opportunity to play with language and story structure and help them to see the possibilities language offers to them. The tales are also ideal for reading aloud, but it seems to me a shame to read them because they are so easily learned.

Stories with a Cumulative Pattern

Like *The Old Woman and the Rice Thief* outlined above, "Crystal Rooster" is a traditional cumulative tale. The following version appears in *Italian Folktales*, selected and edited by Italo Calvino.

Crystal Rooster

There was once a rooster that went strutting about the world. He found a letter lying in the road, picked it up with his beak, and read:

Crystal Rooster, Crystal Hen, Countess Goose, Abbess Duck, Goldfinch Birdie: Let's be off to Tom Thumb's wedding.

The rooster set out in that direction, and shortly met the hen.

"Where are you going, brother rooster?"

"I'm going to Tom Thumb's wedding!"

"May I come, too?"

"If you're mentioned in the letter." He unfolded the letter again and read: Crystal Rooster, Crystal Hen.

"*Here* you are, here you are, so let's be on our way!"

They continued onward together. Before long they met the goose.

"Oh, sister hen and brother rooster! Where are you going?"

"We are going to Tom Thumb's wedding!"

"May I come, too?"

"If you're mentioned in the letter." The rooster unfolded the letter again and read: Crystal Rooster, Crystal Hen, Countess Goose.

"*Here* you are, so let's be on our way!"

The three of them walked and walked and soon met the duck.

"Where are you going, sister goose, sister hen, and brother rooster?"

"We are going to Tom Thumb's wedding!"

"May I come, too?"

"Yes, indeed, if you are mentioned here." He read: Crystal Rooster, Crystal Hen, Countess Goose, Abbess Duck . . .

"You're here all right, so join us!"

Before long they met the goldfinch birdie.

"Where are you going, sister duck, sister goose, sister hen, and brother rooster?"

"We are going to Tom Thumb's wedding!"

"May I come, too?"

"Yes, indeed, if you're mentioned here!" He unfolded the letter again: Crystal Rooster, Crystal Hen, Countess Goose, Abbess Duck, Goldfinch Birdie.

"*You* are here too."

So all five of them walked on together.

Lo and behold, they met the wolf, who also asked where they were going.

"We are going to Tom Thumb's wedding," replied the rooster.

"May I come, too?"

"Yes, if you're mentioned here!"

The rooster reread the letter, but it made no mention of the wolf.

"But I want to come!" said the wolf.

Out of fear they all replied, "All right, let's all go."

26

They'd not gone far when the wolf suddenly said, "I'm hungry."

The rooster replied, "I've nothing to offer you."

"I'll just eat you, then!" He opened his mouth wide and swallowed the rooster whole.

Further on he again said, "I'm hungry."

The hen gave him the same answer as the rooster had, and the wolf gobbled her up too. And the goose and the duck went the same way.

Now there was just the wolf and the birdie. The wolf said, "Birdie, I'm hungry!" "And what do you expect me to give you?" "I'll just eat you, then!"

He opened his mouth wide . . . and the bird perched on his head. The wolf tried his best to catch him, but the bird flitted all around, hopped from branch to branch, then back to the wolf's head and on to his tail, driving him to distraction.

When the wolf was completely exhausted, he spied a woman coming down the road with the reapers' lunch in a basket on her head. The bird called to the wolf, "If you spare my life, I'll see that you get the hearty meal of noodles and meat which that woman is bringing the reapers. As soon as she sees me, she'll want to catch me. I'll fly off and hop from branch to branch. She'll put her basket down and come after me. Then you can go and eat everything up."

That's just what happened. The woman came up, spied the beautiful little bird, and immediately reached out to catch him. He then flew off a little way, and she put down her basket and ran after him. So the wolf approached the basket and started eating.

"Help! Help!" screamed the woman.

The reapers came running with scythes and sticks, pounced upon the wolf, and killed him. Out of his belly, safe and sound, hopped crystal rooster, crystal hen, countess goose, abbess duck, and together with goldfinch birdie they all went to Tom Thumb's wedding.

Sometimes, cumulative stories are referred to as *chain tales* due to the chain of events that they describe. Often, but not always, there are recurring lines or refrains which give the storyteller time to think about the next link in the chain, making this very common type of story easy to learn. In the Russian tale, "The Magic Swan Geese," we can see these features at work. The swan geese referred to are magical birds, possibly created by the folklore figure, Baba Yaga. This version of the story appears in Afanas'ev's *Russian Fairy Tales*.

The Magic Swan Geese

Once upon a time there lived a family, a man, a woman and their two children, a girl and a boy.

"Daughter, daughter!" said the woman one day. "We are going to work. We shall bring you back a bun, sew you a dress, and buy you a handkerchief. Be careful! Watch over your baby brother. Do not leave the house."

When the parents had gone, the daughter forgot what they told her. She put her brother in the grass outside the window and ran off to play. Some magic swan geese came, seized the little brother, and carried him off on their wings.

The girl came back and found her brother gone. She gasped. She rushed to look in every corner, but she could not find him. She called him, wept and lamented that her mother and father would scold her severely. Still her little brother did not answer.

She ran into the open field. The swan geese flashed in the distance and vanished behind the dark forest.

It was well known that the swan geese had stolen many children. The girl guessed they had stolen her brother. She rushed after them. She ran and ran and saw a stove.

"Stove, stove, tell me whither have the geese flown?"

"If you eat my cake of rye, I will tell you."

"Oh, in my parent's house we don't even eat cakes of wheat." The stove did not tell her.

She ran further and saw an apple tree.

"Apple tree, apple tree, tell me, whither have the geese flown?"

"If you eat one of my apples, I will tell you."

"Oh, in my parent's house we don't eat apples." The apple tree did not tell her.

She ran further and saw a river of milk with shores of pudding.

"River of milk, shores of pudding, tell me, whither have the geese flown?"

"If you eat my simple pudding with milk, I will tell you."

"Oh, in my parent's house we don't even eat cream." The river of milk did not tell her.

She ran further and saw a prickly hedgehog.

"Hedgehog, hedgehog, tell me whither have the geese flown?"

"Thither," he said and pointed.

She ran and saw a little hut that stood on chicken legs and turned round and round. On the roof, the geese slept with their heads tucked under their wings. In the hut dozed Baba Yaga with her veined snout and clay legs, and her little brother was sitting on a bench playing with golden apples.

She crept in, seized her little brother and ran out. But the geese awoke and gave chase. Where could she hide? There flowed the river of milk with shores of pudding.

"River of milk, shores of pudding, hide me!"

"If you eat my simple pudding with milk, I will hide you."

She ate it and the river hid her beneath the shore as the geese flew by. She went out, said "thank you," and ran on carrying her brother. The geese turned back and saw her. Where would she hide?

There was the apple tree.

"Apple tree, apple tree, hide me!"

"If you eat one of my apples, I will hide you." She ate it quickly and the apple tree folded its branches over them and sheltered them beneath its leaves. The geese flew by.

She went out again and ran on with her brother. The geese turned again and saw her. The geese swooped down. They began to beat her with their wings. At any moment they would tear her baby brother from her arms. Where could she hide?

There was the stove.

"Stove, stove, hide me!"

"If you eat my cake of rye, I will hide you." She quickly stuck the cake in her mouth, crawled into the stove, and sat there.

The geese whirred and whirred. They quacked and quacked. Finally, they flew away without their prey.

The girl ran home with her baby brother and it was a good thing she came when she did for soon afterward her mother and father came back.

Some cumulative tales are called swapping tales because of the way ideas are linked. Sometimes I call them windshield-wiper tales because they swing back and forth between questions and answers. If you look back to the nursery rhyme "Burnie's Hill" in chapter 1 you will notice that it is a back-and-forth sequence. Similarly, there are alternating scenes in "King Nimrod's Tower" (in chapter 3) and before-and-after sequences, such as in "The Travels of a Fox," below.

The Travels of a Fox

A fox digging behind a stump found a bumblebee. The fox put the bumblebee in his bag, and traveled.

The first house he came to he went in, and said to the mistress of the house, "Can I leave my bag here while I go to Squintum's?"

"Yes," said the woman.

"Then be careful not to open the bag," said the fox.

But as soon as the fox was out of sight, the woman just took a little peep into the bag, and out flew the bumblebee, and the rooster caught him and ate him all up.

After a while the fox came back. He took up his bag, and he saw that his bumblebee was gone, and he said to the woman, "Where is my bumblebee?"

And the woman said, "I just untied the string, and the bumblebee flew out, and the rooster ate him up."

"Very well," said the fox. "I must have the rooster, then." So he caught the rooster and put him in his bag, and traveled.

And the next house he came to he went in, and said to the mistress of the house, "Can I leave my bag here while I go to Squintum's?"

"Yes," said the woman.

"Then be careful not to open the bag," said the fox.

But as soon as the fox was out of sight the woman just took a little peep into the bag, and the rooster flew out, and the pig caught him and ate him all up.

After a while the fox came back. He took up his bag, and he saw that his rooster was gone, and he said to the woman, "Where is my rooster?"

And the woman said, "I just untied the string, and the rooster flew out, and the pig ate him up."

"Very well," said the fox. "I must have the pig, then."

So he caught the pig and put him in his bag, and traveled.

And the next house he came to he went in, and said to the mistress of the house, "Can I leave my bag here while I go to Squintum's?"

"Yes," said the woman.

"Then be careful not to open the bag," said the fox.

But as soon as the fox was out of sight the woman just took a little peep into the bag, and the pig jumped out, and the ox gored him.

After a while the fox came back. He took up his bag, and he saw that his pig was gone, and he said to the woman, "Where is my pig?"

And the woman said, "I just untied the string, and the pig jumped out, and the ox gored him."

"Very well," said the fox. "I must have the ox, then."

So he caught the ox and put him in his bag, and traveled.

And the next house he came to he went in, and said to the mistress of the house, "Can I leave my bag here while I go to Squintum's?"

"Yes," said the woman.

"Then be careful not to open the bag," said the fox.

But as soon as the fox was out of sight the woman just took a little peep, and the ox got out, and the woman's little boy broke off his horns and killed him.

After a while the fox came back. He took up his bag, and he saw that his ox was gone, and he said to the woman, "Where is my ox?"

And the woman said, "I just untied the string, and the ox got out, and my little boy broke off his horns and killed him."

"Very well," said the fox. "I must have the little boy, then."

So he caught the little boy and put him in his bag, and traveled.

And the next house he came to he went in, and said to the mistress of the house, "Can I leave my bag here while I go to Squintum's?"

"Yes," said the woman.

"Then be careful not to open the bag," said the fox.

The woman was making cake, and her children were around her, teasing for it.

"Oh, ma, give me a piece!" said one, and "Oh, ma, give me a piece!" said the others.

And the smell of the cake came to the little boy weeping and crying in the bag, and he heard the children beg for the cake, and he said, "Oh, mammy, give me a piece!"

Then the woman opened the bag and took the little boy out, and she put the house-dog in the bag in the little boy's place. And the little boy stopped crying and joined the other children.

After a while the fox came back. He took up his bag, and he saw that it was tied fast, and he put it on his back, and traveled deep into the woods. Then he sat down and untied the bag, and if the little boy had been in the bag things would have gone badly with him.

But the little boy was safe at the woman's house, and when the fox untied the bag the house-dog jumped out and caught the fox and killed him.

In addition to the recurring lines and refrains, and the clear scene-by-scene sequences of these highly patterned tales, the ancient Rule of Three (three sons, three daughters, three wishes, three tries, three magic objects) is another memory device the storyteller can call upon to master the tale. In the story "Tipingee" from Diane Wolkstein's *The Magic Orange Tree*, note how many times three of something occurs.

Tipingee

"I'm Tipingee,
She's Tipingee,
We're Tipingee, too."

There was once a girl named Tipingee who lived with her stepmother. Her father was dead. The stepmother was selfish, and even though she lived in the girl's house she did not like to share what she earned with the girl.

One morning, the stepmother was cooking sweets to sell in the market. The fire under her pot went out. Tipingee was in school, so the stepmother had to go herself into the forest to find more firewood. She walked for a long time, but she did not find any wood. She continued walking. Then she came to a place where there was firewood everywhere. She gathered it into a bundle. But it was too heavy to lift up onto her head. Still, she did not want anyone else to have any of the firewood. So standing in the middle of the forest she cried out:

"My friends, there is so much wood here and at home I have no wood. Where can I find a person who will help me carry the firewood?"

Suddenly an old man appeared. "I will help you to carry the firewood. But then what will you give me?"

"I have very little," the woman said, "but I will find something to give you when we get to my house."

The old man carried the firewood for the stepmother, and when they got to the house he said, "I have carried the firewood for you. Now what will you give me?"

"I will give you a servant girl. I will give you my stepdaughter, Tipingee."

Now Tipingee was in the house, and when she heard her name she ran to the door and listened.

"Tomorrow I will send my stepdaughter to the well at noon for water. She will be wearing a red dress, call her by her name, Tipingee, and she will come to you. Then you can take her."

"Very well," said the man, and he went away.

Tipingee ran to her friends. She ran to the houses of all the girls in her class and asked them to wear red dresses the next day.

At noon the next day the old man went to the well. He saw one little girl dressed in red. He saw a second little girl dressed in red. He saw a third little girl dressed in red.

"Which of you is Tipingee?" he asked.

The first little girl said: "I'm Tipingee."

The second little girl said: "She's Tipingee."

The third little girl said: "We're Tipingee, too."

"Which of you is Tipingee?" asked the old man.

Then the little girls began to clap and jump up and down and chant:

I'm Tipingee,

She's Tipingee,

We're Tipingee, too.

I'm Tipingee,

She's Tipingee,

We're Tipingee, too.

Rah! The old man went to the woman and said: "You tricked me. All the girls were dressed in red and each one said she was Tipingee."

"That is impossible," said the stepmother. "Tomorrow she will wear a black dress. Then you will find her. The one wearing a black dress will be Tipingee. Call her and take her."

But Tipingee heard what her stepmother said and ran and begged all her friends to wear black dresses the next day.

When the old man went to the well the next day, he saw one little girl dressed in black. He saw a second little girl dressed in black. He saw a third little girl dressed in black.

"Which of you is Tipingee?" he asked.

The first little girl said: "I'm Tipingee."

The second little girl said: "She's Tipingee."

The third little girl said: "We're Tipingee, too."

"Which of you is Tipingee?" asked the old man.

And the girls joined hands and skipped about and sang:

I'm Tipingee,

She's Tipingee,

We're Tipingee, too.

I'm Tipingee,

She's Tipingee,

We're Tipingee, too.

The man was getting angry. He went to the stepmother and said, "You promised to pay me and you are only giving me problems. You tell me Tipingee and everyone here is Tipingee, Tipingee, Tipingee, Tipingee. If this happens a third time, I will come and take you for my servant."

"My dear sir," said the stepmother, "tomorrow she will be in yellow, completely in yellow, call her and take her."

And again Tipingee ran and told her friends to dress in yellow.

At noon the next day, the old man arrived at the well. He saw one little girl dressed in yellow. He saw a second little girl dressed in yellow. He saw a third little girl dressed in yellow.

"Which of you is Tipingee?" he asked.

The first little girl said: "I'm Tipingee."

The second little girl said: "She's Tipingee."

The third little girl said: "We're Tipingee, too."

"Which of you is Tipingee?" the old man shouted.

But the girls just clapped and jumped up and down and sang:

I'm Tipingee,

She's Tipingee,

We're Tipingee, too.
I'm Tipingee,
She's Tipingee,
We're Tipingee, too.

The old man knew he would never find Tipingee. He went to the stepmother and took her away. When Tipingee returned home, she was gone. So she lived in her own house with all her father's belongings, and she was happy.

A common element in cumulative tales is the journey. A crisis necessitates that someone make a journey to bring back a special object or gain important advice or knowledge. In the course of the journey, the main character often has to surmount tricky obstacles and deal with powerful forces. This Azerbaijan tale is an example.

The Loafer

There was once a man who was so lazy that his wife and children went hungry most of the time. Day after day he loafed around without so much as lifting a finger. His wife pleaded with him to get a job. And the man would say, "Don't worry. We are going to be very rich. Be patient."

Well, the wife was patient. The children were patient. But nothing happened. They were as poor as ever. One day the wife lost her patience.

"We're going to starve to death," she said. "Go find a wise man. Ask him how we can stop being poor."

The man agreed to go and was soon on his way. He walked, walked, walked for three days and three nights. On the fourth day he met a scrawny wolf.

"Where are you going?" snarled the wolf.

"To a wise man to ask his advice on how to become rich without having to work."

"Perhaps he can tell you what I am to do to get well. Day and night I have pains in my stomach that give me no peace. Two long years I have suffered."

"Very well," said the man. "I'll ask him about it."

The man walked, walked, walked for three days and three nights and came to an apple tree growing by the roadside.

"Where are you going?" the apple tree asked him.

"To a wise man to ask his advice on how to get rich without having to work."

"Perhaps he can tell you what I am to do to get well. Every spring I bloom but the blossoms wither and die and I bear no fruit."

"Very well," said the man. "I'll ask him about it."

The man walked, walked, walked for three days and three nights and came to a large lake.

All of a sudden a big fish thrust his head above the water.

"Where are you going?" burbled the fish.

"To a wise man to ask his advice on how I can get rich without working."

"Perhaps he can tell you what I am to do to get well. For six long years I have suffered a sharp pain in my throat."

"Very well," said the man, "I'll ask him about it."

The man walked, walked, walked for three days and three nights and came to a place where many rose bushes grew. Under one of them sat an old man with a long grey beard.

"Are you the wise man I have been to find?" asked the man.

"Yes, I am. Tell me quickly what you want of me."

The lazy man said, "I want to know how I can get rich without working."

"Is there nothing else you want to ask?" said the wise man.

"There is," said the man and he told the wise man what the wolf, the apple tree, and the fish wanted of him.

"A large gem is lodged in the throat of the fish. The fish will be cured as soon as the gem is removed," replied the wise man.

"As for the tree, a large jug filled with silver coins is buried under its roots. The tree will bear fruit again once the jug is dug out. In order for the wolf to be cured he must swallow the first lazy loafer who comes along."

"And what about my request?" asked the man.

"What you wish for has already been granted. Return to your family."

The lazy man was overjoyed. He started home without another word. He walked, walked, walked until he came to the lake where the fish was waiting for him.

"Has the wise man told you what I am to do?" it asked.

"A gem is lodged in your throat. Take it out and you will be well again," said the man, and he turned to go.

"Help me!" cried the fish. "Take the gem out of my throat. You will have cured me and gotten the gem for yourself."

"Why should I?" said the man. "I'm going to become rich without lifting a finger."

And with these words he turned and walked and walked and walked until he came to the apple tree.

At the sight of the man the apple tree's limbs trembled. Its leaves rustled with excitement.

"Has the wise man told you what I am to do?" it asked.

"Yes, he has," said the man. "A large jug of silver coins lies buried under your roots. As soon as it is dug out you will bear fruit again."

And with these words the man turned to go.

"Please!" cried the tree. "Dig out the jug. You will be helping yourself too. The silver will be yours."

"Why should I?" replied the man. "The wise man told me I'd be rich without doing anything."

And the man walked away. He walked and walked and walked until he met the scrawny wolf.

"Did the wise man tell you what I am to do?" asked the wolf trembling with impatience. "Quickly, tell me at once."

"Swallow the first lazy loafer who comes along," replied the man.

The wolf thanked the man and then asked what he had seen and heard on the journey. The man told the wolf about the apple tree and the fish and what they had asked of him.

"But I didn't bother with them for I'm going to be rich without doing any work."

The wolf listened and was overjoyed.

"Well, well," he thought. "I need not search for a loafer. The loafer has come to me."

And the wolf pounced on the man and swallowed him on the spot.

Another highly patterned tale is the infinity story or endless tale. In chapter 1 I mentioned "Pete and Repete" and one or two others. Many children meet these tales in songs such as "Michael Finnigan." Look for "The Fox and the Geese" in *Grimm's Tales for Young and Old*, translated by Ralph Manheim.

Some Formula Tales You Might Want to Tell

CHAIN TALES

1. "The Old Woman and Her Pig," in *English Fairy Tales* collected by Joseph Jacobs
2. "The Hedgehog's Waistcoat," in *The Faber Storybook* edited by Kathleen Lines
3. *The Fat Cat*, by Jack Kent
4. "The Turnip," in *Russian Fairy Tales* collected by Aleksandr Afanas'ev
5. "Sody Sallyratus," in *Grandfather Tales* collected and retold by Richard Chase

TALES WITH REPETITIVE LANGUAGE OR SEQUENCES

1. *Over in the Meadow*, by John Langstaff
2. *A Dark, Dark Tale*, by Ruth Brown
3. *Something from Nothing*, by Phoebe Gilman
4. "Soap, Soap, Soap," in *Grandfather Tales* collected and retold by Richard Chase
5. *Brown Bear, Brown Bear, What Do You See?*, Bill Martin, Jr.

TALES WITH REFRAINS OR CHANTS

1. "The China Spaniel," in *The Wonder Dog* by Richard Hughes
2. "Grey Goat," in *A Bag of Moonshine* by Alan Garner
3. "The Gold in the Chimley," in *World Folktales* edited by Atelia Clarkson and Gilbert B. Cross
4. "The Cat and the Mouse," in *To Read and to Tell* chosen and edited by Norah Montgomerie
5. "The Strange Visitor," in *English Fairy Tales* collected by Joseph Jacobs

JOURNEY TALES

1. *The Mouse Bride*, by Monica Chang
2. "The Magic Drum," in *Ten Small Tales* by Celia Lottridge
3. *The Little White Hen*, by Anita Hewett
4. *The Dream Eater,* by Christian Garrison
5. "The Lad Who Went to the North Wind," in *East o' the Sun and West o' the Moon* translated by George Webbe Dasent

Key Anthologies of Traditional Stories

To assist you further, I highly recommend that you explore the following anthologies of traditional stories.

- *Ten Small Tales*, by Celia Lottridge
  This outstanding collection of tales contains traditional material from many lands which goes beyond familiar early childhood stories such as The Three Bears. Lottridge, who is both an accomplished oral performer and a writer, has retold stories which bear the magic properties of old favorites yet will be shiny new to most listeners. In her notes the author says, "I have shaped the stories by telling them to many groups of children, giving special attention to the elements of the story that encourage listeners to participate with their voices or their bodies."

- *The Brothers Grimm: Popular Folk Tales*, translated by Brian Alderson
  This excellent anthology includes thirty-one of the tales collected by Jacob and Wilhelm Grimm. Many of them are familiar but others such as "The Blue Light" and "The Merry Tale of the Clever Little Tailor" are less well known. Brian Alderson, who translated the stories, notes in the Afterword: "I have tried to bring into my English texts something of the unselfconscious directness and the colloquial ease which are characteristic of the Marchen at their best. Where the original is very close to an oral mode — especially in dialect stories — I have tried to retain this in English; and where there are more 'literary' effects and embellishments I have still tried to give a fluency to the story which will make it pleasant to read aloud."

- *A Bag of Moonshine*, by Alan Garner
  In the beginning of this highly entertaining collection of English and Welsh traditional tales, Alan Garner features this quote by John Maruskin: "— it is in the speech of canters and housewives, in the speech of blacksmiths and old women, that one discovers the magic that sings the claim of the voice in the shadow, or that chants the rhyme of the fish in the well."

  Garner does indeed have an ear for "the claim of the voice in the shadow," thus creating another book which reads aloud well. Many of the stories are about fools and funny folk, but there are sensitive thought-provoking ones too. See also his *Book of British Fairy Tales*.

- *English Fairy Tales*, collected by Joseph Jacobs
These wonderful stories from England and lowland Scotland were collected in the nineteenth century by folklorist Joseph Jacobs and recorded in such a way that they read aloud brilliantly. So popular has this collection become that over the years illustrators have retold the stories again and again. Compilers of anthologies have dipped into the collection endlessly.

   No one who wants to learn and tell stories should be without this valuable resource.

- *The Old Wives Fairy Tale Book*, edited by Angela Carter
Many of the stories in this first-rate anthology will also be well suited to teenagers and adults.

   The late English novelist, Angela Carter, who had a keen interest in the traditional tale, has assembled tales from around the world which all feature female protagonists, "be they clever or brave, or good or silly or cruel or heroic or awesomely unfortunate." In her introduction, Carter explains, "I've tried as far as possible, to avoid stories that have been conspicuously 'improved' by collectors, or rendered 'literary', and I haven't rewritten any myself, however great the temptation, or collated two versions, or even cut anything, because I wanted to keep a sense of many different voices."

   See also her *Second Virago Book of Fairy Tales*.

- *The Magic Orange Tree*, by Diane Wolkstein
This very special anthology of stories was collected by storyteller Diane Wolkstein during several visits to the island of Haiti during the 1970s. Accompanying the stories is a splendid introduction which describes the background and the task faced by the compiler in assembling the material. In addition, before each story we are told about the telling of the story in its natural setting. Many of the twenty-seven stories include a song or chorus which can be used to involve the listener. Musical scores for the songs are provided.

   The appearance of these stories on sound recordings and in new anthologies is a testament to their power and impact. Stories such as "The Name" I have shared with preschoolers in the morning and senior English students in the afternoon with equally splendid results. The popular tale "Owl" is here as well as many other stories of laughter, mystery, and suspense. There are wonderful surprises to be discovered in this collection, now in print again.

- *The People Could Fly: American Black Folktales*, told by Virginia Hamilton

  Virginia Hamilton is an outstanding writer and *The People Could Fly* is a stirring tribute to the powers of imagination of enslaved Africans who, as Hamilton points out, "were forced to live without citizenship, without rights, as property — like horses and cows — belonging to someone else." Here are trickster tales, ghost stories and devil tales, riddles, laughter and tales of freedom — twenty-four in all retold in simple direct language but resonant of the voices of far-off tellers. These selections beg to become stories on the breath.

  See also Hamilton's *In The Beginning: Creation Stories from around the World*.

- *Old Peter's Russian Tales*, by Arthur Ransome

  I continue to go back to this collection even though I have other sources of Russian folk and fairy tales. Ransome retold these stories over seventy years ago and his engaging format, along with the strong and exciting tales he chose to present, have undoubtedly contributed to the book's longevity and popularity.

  A second collection of Ransome stories, *War of the Birds and the Beasts*, was gathered by Hugh Brogan from manuscripts prepared by Ransome but never published. Some of these tales would be appropriate for older children. One of my favorites is "The Little Cattle" which I heard Toronto storyteller Lynda Howes tell brilliantly.

- *Bury My Bones But Keep My Words: African Tales for Retelling* by Tony Fairman

  In this unusual but very entertaining collection, Tony Fairman has created a context for the thirteen stories which come from several African countries. He has set the stories up for retelling by showing how they might be performed. "I've tried to describe people and places in Africa where the tales are being told. I've described night time in Africa, the houses, the parents and children, the weather, the sights, sounds and smells you would notice if you were there listening to the tales. I've written songs you can sing, just as Africans sing with a chorus and lead singer. And I've shown how the listeners behave during the tale: how they sing, move and ask questions. Everybody joins in, helping the tale to come out." The stories are mostly traditional but Fairman has included contemporary ones as well.

■ *Tales of Magic and Enchantment*, by Kathleen Lines
Included in this fine old collection is a selection of fairytales and legends from different national traditions. Among the thirteen fairytales are some that will not be widely known. "The Feather of Finist the Falcon" (Russia) and "How the Raja's Son Won the Princess Labam" (India) are examples. Attention then shifts to tales from the prose cycles and poems of medieval literature. Sources here include the Old Testament, Chaucer's *Canterbury Tales*, the Irish hero tales, and the story of Beowulf. These latter extracts all serve as a good introduction to the hero tales and romantic legends.

■ *The Illustrated Book of Fairy Tales*, by Neil Philip
For nearly the same price as a current highly illustrated anthology of about eight stories you can obtain this collection of more than fifty retold by Neil Philip. Philip has published many fine collections of myth and folklore including *The Cinderella Story*, *The Penguin English Folk Tales*, and *The Penguin Scottish Folk Tales*. In this collection, not only do you get the tales, but you will find considerable background information both in photos, illustrations, and text on the history of the fairytale. If I have any quibble, it is that at times some of the stories seem to have been reduced to information. That criticism aside, this book is well worth finding.

There are two additional works I would like to mention. Storyteller/ anthologist Eileen Colwell and Ruth Manning Saunders have contributed extensively to the gathering of stories. For the most part their choices are impeccable, but in each instance certain of their works have appealed to me more than others. In the case of Eileen Colwell I strongly recommend *Humblepuppy*, a collection of traditional and contemporary stories. From among the many works of Ruth Manning Saunders, try *A Book of Magic Animals*, folktales from around the world featuring creatures both real and imaginary.

Recommended Anthologies of Contemporary Stories

Although the purpose of this survey of anthologies has been to assist you in finding traditional material, there are three highly recommended collections of contemporary stories: *The Wonder Dog* by Richard Hughes, *How the Whale Became and Other Stories* by Ted Hughes, and *Tales of the Early World*, also by Ted Hughes.

- *The Wonder Dog*, by Richard Hughes
  It could be argued that the stories of Richard Hughes were born of the oral tradition. In the foreword we learn that the stories written down were only a few of many told and that they survived because a listener told them back.

  The Wonder Dog contains eighteen of the twenty stories first published in *The Spider's Palace* (1931) and ten of the thirteen stories from *Don't Blame Me* (1940). If the ability to make a story compelling and memorable is the work of a gifted storyteller, then Hughes's work qualifies. I have told many of these modern fairytales including "The China Spaniel," "The Ants," "The Spider's Palace," and "The Jungle School"; they have been a joy to learn and to tell. In his review of this collection Geoffrey Parker said, *"The Wonder Dog* will stand in the open market as 180 pages of enthralling stories for children between the ages of five and ten. For this, we — and they — can Be Glad." I would add that a large number of teenagers and adults have been "Glad" also.

- *How the Whale Became and Other Stories*, by Ted Hughes
  Once I was asked to tell a *trickster tale* as part of a storytelling festival. I turned immediately to poet Ted Hughes's *How the Whale Became*. There were several suitable stories in this collection, but I settled on "Why Owl Behaves as He Does." Among the traditional tricksters, Anansi, Raven, and The Hodja, Owl stood up extremely well.

  Although the stories may simply be explained away as modern *pourquoi tales* these sinewy narratives, like folktales, hold up to the light the selfishness, meanness, foolishness, and vanity of humankind.

- *Tales of the Early World*, by Ted Hughes
  Twenty-five years after the publication of *How the Whale Became*, Hughes picked up where he left off and released *Tales of the Early*

World, a collection of remarkable creation stories which I have found entertain adults as well as children.

Other Recommended Sources of Stories from around the World

Anancy-Spiderman, by James Berry

The Answered Prayer and Other Yemenite Folktales, by Sharlya Gold and Mishael Maswari Caspi

Best Loved Folktales of the World, by Joanna Cole

The Ch'l-Lin Purse: A Collection of Ancient Chinese Stories, by Linda Fang

A Circle Long Ago: A Treasury of Native Lore from North America, by Nancy Van Laan

The Cow Tail Switch and Other West African Stories, by Harold Courlander and George Herzog

Cric Crac: A Collection of West Indian Stories, by Grace Hallworth

The Dreamer Awakes, by Alice Kane

Fairy Tales of Ireland, by William Butler Yeats

Favorite Folktales from around the World, by Jane Yolen

Fearless Girls, Wise Women & Beloved Sisters — Heroines in Folk Tales from around the World, by Kathleen Ragan

The Girl Who Dreamed Only Geese and Other Tales of the Far North, by Howard Norman

Mysterious Tales of Japan, by Rafe Martin

Next Teller: A Book of Canadian Storytelling, by Dan Yashinsky

The Rainbow People, by Laurence Yep

Scottish Traditional Tales, by A. J. Bruford and D. A. Macdonald

Seasons of Splendour: Tales, Myths and Legends of India, by Madhur Jaffrey

Tales for the Telling: Irish Folk and Fairy Stories, by Edna O'Brien

Tales from Gold Mountain: Stories of the Chinese in the New World, by Paul Yee

Twenty Tellable Tales: Audience Participation Stories for the Beginning Storyteller, by Margaret R. MacDonald

The Young Oxford Book of Folk Tales, by Kevin Crossley-Holland

Many beautifully illustrated retellings of folk and fairy tales are available in school and public libraries. For those with little time to page through anthologies, these books can make selection easier.

 THREE

Making a Story Your Own

I am just this one.
Nobody else makes the words
I shape with sound when I talk.

From *When I Dance* by James Berry

Storytelling is about the art of improvisation, not imitation. The story-tellers of old were seldom parrots who re-created stories in assembly-line fashion. Each teller brought his or her imagination to bear on the story. You need only look at all the variants of Rumpel-stiltskin to glimpse the possibilities.

Each of us must learn a story in our own way, but when it comes to making it our own, each story will place its demands on us. Some people learn best by listening. Repeated listenings to a tape-recorded story serves them well. Some may prefer to write the story out in full, jot down a plot summary, or draw the story in a storyboard fashion. Several slow readings over a period of time will do for others.

Regardless of how a story is approached, memorizing a plot is *not* storytelling. Stories are about people, ideas, and feelings. Telling a story calls for remembering, identifying, and interpreting. It is about improvising, exploring, experimenting, and engaging in the life of the story. Preparing to tell might best be described as a building process.

When you set out to make a story yours, you must discover more about the story than you ever deemed possible. Extensive research yields one kind of learning, but that isn't what I am referring to. What I have in mind is the kind of imaginative exploration that takes you into every nook and cranny of the story.

Even though the art of storytelling is extremely personal and subjective, some fundamentals characterize good practice. Knowing your story well is the first of them.

Learning the Story

Having a firm grasp of what the story is about and a good knowledge of its form or structure is essential to the fluency you bring to the telling. Using Jan Knappert's short tale, "The Bamboo Tower," which appears in *Myths and Legends of the Congo*, let's walk through some of the steps you might take.

Read the story very slowly, much slower than you normally would.

The Bamboo Tower

This story is an old Congolese version of the tale of the tower of Babel. The same story is found among the Bakongo and the Baluba.

The Lendu are very stupid people, say the Alur. One night as they gazed at the stars, they suddenly arrived at a very important conclusion, so they ran and communicated it to their king: "We have realized that all those lights up there must prove that it is a prosperous country, in which many people can afford to keep their fires burning all night. We would therefore advise Your Majesty to build a tower up to the sky so that we can go and learn from those people."

The king ordered that thousands of bamboo poles be cut, and hauled up to the highest hill in his realm. The first poles were dug into the ground, and cross-beams were tied to them with lianas. On top of this structure further storeys were erected, with diagonal poles and transverse beams for reinforcement. The king kept control of progress on top so that he rose up with every new storey. He wanted to be the first to set foot on the sky.

The chief minister, Ledza, was in charge at the bottom end. He directed the transportation of supplies. After nine months he noticed that the bamboo poles at the bottom were beginning to rot. The whole structure was beginning to sway unsteadily. With great courage and perseverance, minister Ledza climbed up all the stairs and ladders that had been constructed in those nine months, to see the king and warn him that his tower was tottering. The king merely said: "Ledza, you are a liar, go back!" He could not be convinced that something had to be done, as he was constantly looking up at the sky, expecting all the time to reach it with the next storey. "Go back to your duties, don't bother me with the problems of the earth, don't you see I am trying to meet God?"

The minister Ledza gave up, climbed down and ran away just in time. The whole tower tottered and collapsed in one terrifying crash! All the builders perished and only the minister Ledza escaped.

Today there is still a lake on Mount Ju, surrounded by bamboo. It bears witness to the lack of intelligence of the Lendu people, according to the Alur.

Now repeat your slow reading two or three times till you feel confident you have the gist of the story. Then set the story aside and make a brief plot summary or capture the story in six to eight sketches.

Learning the Plot

It's important when learning a story to distance yourself from the language of the text. You don't want to memorize it. You want to get the story into your own words. Making a plot outline such as mine below will help you do this.

1. Lendu people think stars in sky are fires of a prosperous country.
2. Lendu people convince king to build a tower to the country above.
3. King orders thousands of bamboo poles to be cut.
4. Tower building begins on highest hill with poles dug into ground.
5. A flimsy structure of cross-beams lashed by vines to diagonal poles is erected.
6. King insists on supervising the job from the top of the tower in order to be first to meet the "sky people."
*7. Nine months later, the chief minister, Ledza, warns the king about rotting base poles.
8. King ignores warning and forges ahead.
9. Ledza barely reaches the ground before tower crashes.
10. Human casualties are catastrophic.
11. Today a bamboo forest grows where once the tower reached toward the sky.

Study your outline to determine where the climax occurs. For me the climax is the moment when I knew how the story is going to end. Here it is marked by a star. Make sure that you have a clear idea of the steps leading up to the climax.

Now put your outline aside and talk the story through to yourself. Talking through the story again and again, not necessarily all at once but over a couple of hours or throughout a day, will help you develop confidence in your work. Go back to the story now and read it again. Check for any significant scenes you might have omitted. This process can take a few minutes for some stories and a few days for others.

As you continue to practise by talking the story out try to see the story in your mind's eye. Linger over some of your mental images. How might you slow the story a bit in order to blend aspects of these images into your tale? Details about the king's appearance or suspenseful moments in Ledza's precarious climb to the top of the tower can enrich your story and give you an opportunity to make it yours — you can cloak the bare bones of the story in the raiment of your imagination.

Knowing when not to speak while telling a story is as important as knowing when you should speak. Where might you pause to enhance your presentation? In "The Bamboo Tower" a pause before the king responds to Ledza could be quite effective.

I have always believed that a love of sound is important to the successful storyteller. The sound and rhythm of words are also part of their meaning and each story directs us through its words to adopt a certain tone of voice and explore the full range of sound and silences that the story offers. Here are some examples of the sounds of language which I recorded from participants at a storytelling workshop. In each instance these were their first attempts to tell the story in their own words:

A. "It was cold. Bitter cold. The people of the Lendu tribe had never experienced such cold. Their suffering was great. Already many old people and young babies had perished from it.

" 'We will most certainly die unless something is done,' the people pleaded.

"Their king gazed hopelessly towards the heavens and then he cried, 'I have noticed that the tribe which inhabits the land above us have many fires which burn throughout the night. Surely a people who can afford to keep fires going throughout the night must enjoy prosperity that can be shared with us. We must try to reach them and ask for help.' "

B.   "It has been said that the Lendu were a foolish people. It has been said that the Lendu lacked the brains to manage their own affairs. But I ask, do you have the courage of the Lendu? Do you have the will to try to make your dreams come true or do you walk always with your eyes down, fearing that you might bear witness to the greatness of others?

     "The Lendu were dreamers and they followed their dreams. Let me tell you about them."

C.   "The people of the Lendu tribe were not the most brilliant who ever lived, but on the whole they lived a peaceful existence and seemed reasonably satisfied with their achievements.

     "There was a king to lead them and he was not given to extravagant schemes or impossible dreams. Furthermore he had a chief minister named Ledza, to give him wise counsel. But a sudden turn of events changed the lives of these people for all time. It all happened this way."

Each approach is unique. The pattern of the story has not been lost, but the tale has been altered to suit the teller. These openings are all very exciting. Each teller has brought something unique to the telling without losing the essence of the story. There is also something in the sounds of the language which I find majestic.

Once you can tell the story from your outline, go back to the source and reread to determine if you have overlooked any significant details.

Creating Characters

Reread "The Bamboo Tower" again with an eye to the characters and emotions and dilemmas they are experiencing.

One of the challenges the storyteller faces in the telling of a tale is how to convey character traits, relationships, motivations, and purpose of the characters in the story in such a way that the listeners can create them in their minds.

I favor trying to understand a character's attitudes by stepping into the character's mind and trying to tell the story from that character's perspective. Doing this frees up the telling splendidly. In the examples that follow, workshop participants chose a character from "The Bamboo Tower" or invented a witness to what was going on and attempted to tell the story as that character remembered it. All their responses were oral.

A. "I knew it was a fool idea the moment I heard it, but I've worked for the king long enough to know that when he makes up his mind to do something he's going to pursue it. What got him going this time was his stargazing and the sorry state of his coffers. . . ."

B. "My name is Ledza, chief minister to the King of the Lendu tribe. My responsibilities have until recently been well within my ability to manage, but I fear now that I am in a situation which has gotten out of hand."

C. "The first light of day has not yet dawned but already my husband has returned to his labors. The torches of the workers form a ribbon of orange along the road leading to the great tower of the Lendu. You see, our king has taken the decision to build this tower to reach the prosperous tribe that inhabits the skies. Each evening we gaze with envy upon their campfires, shivering in the dark as we nurse the few embers which we are permitted. Fuel here is scarce and our king wishes to consult with the powerful sky tribe but to tell you the truth all of this scares me very much. My husband does not let on, but I know he too is filled with fear."

Telling the story from the point of view of another character offers many interesting possibilities for freeing up the story. When you choose your character, be sure to consider the character's intent. Doing so opens up your options for developing the story. For example, if the story is told by a descendant of Chief Minister Ledza, perhaps what emerges is a kind of hero tale. If the story is recalled by a tribesperson of the Lendu, the intent might be to deliver a cautionary tale about the folly of past leaders. Telling a story from another character's point of view is also a terrific way to rehearse your story and build confidence.

Exploring different narrative perspectives can yield unique and personal moments which will help to make the story truly yours. For example, in the story of Rapunzel, attempting to explain the Sorceress's dreams for Rapunzel can help us to understand the Sorceress's response to Rapunzel's revelations about the prince.

Adding Details

Take a moment to look over the original story again. Is there anything in it that you would like to build back into *your* story? For example, would you retain the word "lianas" and risk perplexed faces or simply say "climbing vines"? Every story has its own special sound. It might be found in interesting turns of phrase, special vocabulary such as "lianas," the repetition of certain lines, or a refrain such as *Trip trap, trip trap*.

When you have worked out your opening and closing, memorize them. Openings and closings are very important. A bit of raggedness in the middle won't matter much, but an uncertain start or a muddled conclusion don't make for a satisfying listening experience. Even though you will continue to shape and reshape the story as you practise it, try to keep beginnings and endings well polished.

Consider other editing possibilities that will help you to make the story your own. However, don't let your zeal cause you to ruin the story. Keep asking yourself, "What belongs to the story and what belongs to me?" In other words, where can you impose your ideas while still retaining the heart of the tale?

A particularly interesting text to consult in this regard is *British Folktales: New Versions* by poet and storyteller Kevin Crossley-Holland. In retelling fifty-five stories from the body of British folktales he has demonstrated admirably some of the possibilities open to the teller. In some instances very little has been done other than a little tidying up. For other tales that were recorded in dialect he has rewritten the text in more contemporary style but with the musicality of the language intact. In a few stories, such as "Sea Woman," plot incidents have been rearranged using flashback techniques. "The Small Tooth Dog" is an example of a story transposed from a historical context to a modern one. Other possibilities that Crossley-Holland demonstrates are converting narration to dialogue, adding characters, deleting characters, condensing some aspects of the story and elaborating others. One of the most interesting examples of elaboration in the collection is "Wildman." Another special favorite of mine is "The Green Children."

Although the preceding methods will work for any story you might wish to learn, they are especially well suited to material from the oral tradition. Since there are no definitive versions of folk literature, you should feel free to add your voice to the long list of voices that have made and remade a given tale. In his introduction to *Italian Folktales,* Italo Calvino makes this point succinctly: "The tale is not beautiful if nothing is added to it . . . in other words its value consists in what is woven and rewoven into it. I too have thought of myself as a link in the anonymous chain without end by which folktales are handed down, links that are never merely instruments or passive transmitters, but — and here the proverb meets Benedetto Croces' theory about popular poetry — its real 'authors.' " Sometimes, you need to write, write, write to achieve the effect you want; other times you learn about what works by responding on the fly to your audience.

Working with Literary Tales

If you choose to tell a literary tale you may not feel comfortable taking liberties with an author's text — even if you memorize though, the story will change with you over time. If your aim is to reproduce the work with a fair degree of accuracy but to stop short of memorization, then you might find it useful to chart the piece. I show how this can be done, using Leon Garfield's retelling of the Old Testament story of the Tower of Babel which follows.

King Nimrod's Tower

There was a boy in Babylon who found a dog. It was a jumping, whooping, whirling, biting baby of a dog; and it had no friends. The boy called it "Snap", because it snapped; and the dog called him "Wuf!" because that was all it could say.

"I'll take you home with me," said the boy, "if you learn how to behave."

The dog bit his shoe; and whooped like anything.

"But I'll leave you here in the fields if you don't learn to behave."

The dog bit his trousers; and whooped again.

And all the brickmakers, carpenters, stone-workers, architects and surveyors who were working in the fields, laughed till they were told to stop laughing and get on with their work.

King Nimrod was building a tower. It was to be as high as heaven. The spot had been chosen, the stone fetched, the clay dug and the bricks baked. Ten thousand workmen fetched and carried, fetched and carried, and did as they were told.

"Look!" said the boy to the dog.

"And try to learn something."

"Hurry!" shouted the foremen.

"Hurry along there!"

And the workmen hurried along.

"Lift!" shouted the foremen.

"All together now — lift!"

And the workmen lifted.

"Sit!" shouted the boy to the dog. "Sit down, sir!"

The dog bit his sleeve and tore it; and whooped and whirled away.

It was a stupid dog. Its head was as thick as porridge, and its feet were like plates of mud. It would never learn to behave.

"King Nimrod will be walking into heaven," said the boy, "before I can take you back to Babylon, to sleep beside my bed."

King Nimrod's tower was growing fast. With ropes and hoists and cranes and ladders, it rose on a sweep of pillars and stairs. It was a mile round at the bottom, and already it was half an hour high. King Nimrod came to see it; and the ten thousand workmen stood to attention, one upon each of ten thousand steps. He climbed to the top and looked up at the sky, where heaven was waiting behind the clouds.

"God save King Nimrod!" everyone shouted together; and threw up their hats and handkerchiefs and dinner-bundles, till the tower looked like a tree with blossoms tossed up in the wind. "God save the King!"

King Nimrod shook his head and smiled. Soon he would be as high as heaven, and on a level with God.

"King Nimrod will save God," he said. "If God learns to behave."

There was a crack of lightning and a rumble of thunder; and the King said: "See! God is frightened. He is shaking in His shoes!"

"Bow down!" shouted the foremen. "Bow down to King Nimrod the Great!"

And all ten thousand workmen bowed down as low as dust.

"Down!" shouted the boy to the dog. "Down, sir, down!"

The dog bit his shirt and pranced and danced away.

"King Nimrod will be having supper with the angels," said the boy, "before I can take you back to Babylon, to sleep beside my bed."

Higher and higher rose the tower, till the workmen toiled in the clouds. Eagles stole their sandwiches, and rainbows painted their shirts.

"Stay at work!" shouted the foremen. "Stay at work or King Nimrod will stop your pay!"

And the ten thousand stayed hard at work; with bricks and mortar and heavy stones.

"Stay!" shouted the boy to the dog. "Stay or I'll stop your dinner!"

The dog jumped up and tore his collar; and whooped and whirled away.

"King Nimrod will be wearing God's dressing-gown and slippers," said the boy, "before I can take you back to Babylon, to sleep beside my bed."

And that was exactly what the angels said to God, who was watching the boy and the dog and not minding King Nimrod in the least.

"My slippers? My dressing-gown?" said God. "That cannot be."

"Behold, 0 Lord!" said the angels. "The tower is rising fast. Strike it down while there is still time!"

"But if it falls," said God, "the boy and the dog will be sure to perish under all those bricks and stones."

"Then what is to be done?" asked the angels. "How else is King Nimrod to be kept in his place?"

"How many miles to Babylon?" asked God.

"Three score miles and ten."

"Can I get there by candlelight?" asked God.

"Yes, and back again!"

So the angels lighted a candle and God went down into the fields of

Babylon, where the foremen shouted and the workmen jumped and obeyed.

"Heave!"

And they all heaved.

"Lift!"

And they all lifted.

"Pull!"

And they all pulled.

Then God smiled and crossed His fingers on every tongue.

"Heave!" shouted the foremen.

And they all lifted.

"Pull!" shouted the foremen.

And they all pushed.

"Lift!" shouted the foremen.

Some pushed, some heaved, and some just sat and scratched their heads.

"What is happening?" shouted the foremen. "The tower will never get built!"

The workmen stared.

"What was that he said?"

"It sounded like, I must get a haircut!"

"No — no! It was, will you come to dinner tonight?"

"Never! He said his mother had a new dress!"

"Nonsense! He said, my feet are killing me!"

"You must be deaf! I heard it plain as anything. He said, is it time to go home yet?"

In the twinkling of an eye, and without a single lesson, they were all talking in languages they had never talked before! In Swedish, German, Spanish, Hebrew, Greek, Latin and Japanese . . . though to each and every one, it sounded like plain double Dutch!

In vain the foremen shouted; in vain King Nimrod raged! The workmen heaved bricks where they should have put statues, and dug holes where they should have built stairs. In vain the foremen threatened; in vain King Nimrod stormed.

Nobody could understand them any more. And worse! The workmen couldn't understand each other, so they just downed tools and left.

They left the tower, they left the fields of Babylon, and wandered far and wide. Soon the great tower stood alone, crusted all over with pillars and piped with stairs, like an unfinished pie in the sky.

King Nimrod walked in the fields, as miserable as sin.

"My tower!" he wept. "My beautiful tower that was to have reached heaven! Alas! No more!"

But he could not even understand himself; and he drifted away like the dust. The boy and the dog were left all alone.

"Sit!" said the boy to his dog. "I only want to be your friend."

And the dog sat.

"Stand up!" said the boy to his dog. "I only want to take you home."

And the dog stood up.

"Good!" said the boy. "Now I can take you back to Babylon, and you can sleep beside my bed!"

So they went.

"How did it happen?" marveled the angels, "At last!"

"Because My Kingdom of Heaven is better reached," said God, "by a bridge than by a tower."

If you look first at the structure of the story, you'll notice that, as mentioned earlier, it operates like a windshield wiper, back and forth, back and forth, between scenes of the boy and the dog and scenes of the foremen and workers building Nimrod's Tower. This simple pattern gives us a useful device for tracking the story.

Here is an example of how the story might be examined. As you do any charting, track special vocabulary or turns of phrase that contribute to the story's unique sound.

	Outline for Scene	**Special Words & Phrases**
Scene One	— Boy meets stray pup/pup is playful and disobedient. — Boy offers a home if dog will behave. — Scene ends with dog biting boy's trousers.	"jumping, whooping, whirling, biting baby of a dog"

	Outline for Scene	Special Words & Phrases
Scene Two	— A tower of stones and brick designed to reach heaven being built for King Nimrod — Foremen shout orders at ten thousand workmen to "hurry," to "lift."	— Spot chosen, stone fetched, clay dug, bricks baked — repetition of "fetched and carried"
Scene Three	— Boy orders dog to sit. — Dog bites boy's sleeve. — Dog described — Boy declares: "King Nimrod will be walking into heaven before I can take you home to Babylon, to sleep beside my bed."	— head thick as porridge — feet like plates of mud
Scene Four	— Tower is rising quickly with ropes, hoists, ladders. — King Nimrod comes to inspect; climbs to top and is cheered by the ten thousand workers who throw hats, handkerchiefs into air. — Nimrod utters threat to God. Thunder and lightning bring boast from Nimrod that God fears him. — Foremen order workers to bow down to Nimrod.	— rose on a sweep of pillars and stairs — mile around at the bottom; half an hour high
Scene Five	— Boy orders dog to bow to Nimrod. — Dog bites boy's shirt. — Boy declares: "King Nimrod will be having supper with the angels before I can take you back to Babylon, to sleep beside my bed."	"pranced and danced away"
Scene Six	— Tower continues to rise into the clouds. — Foremen threaten to stop pay if workers don't stay at work.	— eagles stole their sandwiches — rainbows painted their shirts

	Outline for Scene	**Special Words & Phrases**
Scene Seven	— Boy orders dog to stay. — Dog bites and tears his collar. — Boy declares: "King Nimrod will be wearing God's dressing-gown and slippers before I can take you back to Babylon, to sleep beside my bed."	— "whooped and whirled away"

In scene eight we cut away from the boy and the dog and the workers and the tower and go directly to heaven.

	Outline for Scene	**Special Words & Phrases**
Scene Eight	— Angels raise the alarm about Nimrod's tower. They want God to knock it down. — God is concerned about the safety of the boy and the dog. Finally he decides to go to Babylon and see for himself.	— Behold, O Lord, the tower is rising fast. Strike it down while there is still time! — How many miles to Babylon? — Three score miles and ten — Can I get there by candlelight? — Yes, and back again!
Scene Nine	— God descends to the tower site. — Foremen are shouting orders — "heave," "lift," "pull." — God crosses his fingers on every tongue. — Suddenly chaos erupts. Workers do opposite of what foremen want.	— In the twinkling of an eye and without a single lesson they were all talking in languages they had not talked before.

	Outline for Scene	Special Words & Phrases
Scene Nine (cont'd.)	— Foremen shout. King Nimrod rages. Everything is going wrong. — Discouraged workers throw down their tools and leave. — Nimrod looks at his unfinished tower and weeps and wails and finally exits babbling to himself.	— "crusted all over with pillars and piped with stairs, like an unfinished pie in the sky"
Scene Ten	— Boy speaks kindly to the dog and the dog obeys. — Boy declares: "Now I can take you back to Babylon, and you can sleep beside my bed."	
Scene Eleven	— Angels marvel at God's actions and ask for an explanation which God gives.	— "My Kingdom of Heaven is better reached by a bridge than by a tower."

Charting the story allows more of the story's features to reveal themselves. The close reading that the process requires helps the would-be teller tune in to every detail. For example, in common with many traditional tales, "King Nimrod's Tower" has a refrain, which appears at the end of scenes three, five, seven, and ten. ("King Nimrod will . . . to sleep beside my bed.") I love it when a familiar text from another source is embedded in a new context: the use here of the beautiful nursery rhyme "How many miles to Babylon?" as a conversation between God and the angels works extremely well.

I've tried to draw attention to the notion that a story has a unique sound which the teller should try to preserve. Doing so captures the special aura that the story radiates. By noting words and phrases that are worth keeping you get a very strong sense of the sound of "Nimrod's Tower" and for me that sound resonated powerfully with the King James Version of the Old Testament. ("Behold, O Lord"; "Strike it down"; "Alas! No more!")

It's difficult to imagine introducing colloquial language into this tale. Expressions such as "Jeez Wuf, knock it off will you" are simply not part of the story's language patterns. Certainly, I would want to build back in as much of the beautiful alliterative and rhythmical language as I could while still feeling that I had the story in my own words.

Now that I have grasped the story's structure and become attuned to the tale's sound and language, attention to character and incident can follow.

For other literary tales to tell, look for *The Flying Trunk and Other Stories from Andersen*, translated by Naomi Lewis; *Dragon, Dragon* by John Gardner; *The Devil's Storybook* by Natalie Babbitt; *The Little Bookroom* by Eleanor Farjeon; *Fog Hounds, Wind Cat, Sea Mice* by Joan Aiken; and Carl Sandburg's *Rootabaga Stories*.

Personalizing the Story

In taking on a story it is necessary for me to move back and forth between the world of the story and the personal imagery of my own memories, experiences, and dreams. I must see that story in my imagination. I must hear the voices of the characters speaking. I must identify with how the characters are thinking and feeling. I must have some idea of what that story is saying. Having done that, the story is part of me and I am part of it; the language flows freely.

For example, if a character is about to make a decision that will alter the course of his or her life, I will often replay the scene in slow motion in my head, noting physical movements, feelings moment by moment, facial expressions, and tone of voice. This slowing down of the story can help me to understand a dilemma with greater clarity.

Once I have built a strong sense of a story's setting, developed a keen awareness of the attitudes, feelings, and concerns of the characters, noted significant events, and become familiar with beautiful words, recurring expressions, and language patterns appropriate to the story, it's time to talk it out. I say the story out loud to myself, to the mirror. I even mumble it in the aisle at the supermarket. I use my knowledge of the structure, especially the mini-climaxes, to determine the pacing.

After each telling I recommend that you go back to the source. Read the story again until you are satisfied that your rendering of the story serves its author to the best of your ability.

I have tried to stress that the bringing together of the story and the personal imagery of the teller are central. Personalizing the story gives it the sincerity and conviction that make the experience truly memorable for the listener.

Storyteller Diane Wolkstein said of storytelling in Haiti that, where the community knows its body of literature, the storyteller must bring to the telling of a familiar tale a fresh approach. The rules for storytelling in that community are simple, she explained: you must not tamper with the meaning of the story and you must not change the ending; otherwise, you are expected to be very imaginative in your treatment of the story.

Pretty good advice, I'd say.

Fundamentals of Good Storytelling

1. Choice of story matters greatly. Find something you really want to share.
2. Know your story well.
3. Develop a love of the sound of words.
4. Memorize and polish the story opening and closing.
5. Get the story into your own words, while preserving any special phrases and words from the original.
6. Keep asking yourself, "What belongs to the story and what belongs to me?"
7. Become personally involved in the story. Visualize the action, identify with the characters, understand what the story is saying, and when you tell it make everything happen.
8. Throw yourself wholeheartedly into the tale. Live it.

FOUR

And This Is the Way I Tell It

As usual he (Stanley) was full of explanations for everything. "This is a special place for telling stories in," he announced, in front of a huge, round building with a notice outside saying Royal Albert Hall.

"There was this great King called Albert Hall who was better at telling stories than anyone else, which is why he was made King and he used to tell his stories to thousands of people in here, that's why it's got so many seats inside. And once," he went on, his eye caught by writing scrawled in big letters on some boarding outside — SPURS RULE O.K. — ? "once he had a terrible battle with this person called Spurs who came and said he was even better at telling stories and they fought for three days and three nights on that bit of grass there on the other side of the road and at the end, King Albert Hall threw this Spurs person into that lake there."

"Belt up, Stanley," said Ned.

From *The Voyage of QV66*, by Penelope Lively

As I stated in the previous chapter, telling a story is an intensely personal experience. Each and every one of us must assess our individual strengths and capitalize on them. Unlike the imaginary battle between King Albert Hall and that Spurs person to determine who was the better storyteller, the intent of what follows is to consider aspects of good practice which can help you develop and preserve your unique expression of voice and manner and interpretation.

The way in which I would like to share my ideas is in a question and answer format. Over the years I have kept a record of questions that continue to be put to me about storytelling. I am raising those questions here and answering according to what has worked for me and other storytellers with whom I've been associated.

I don't expect you to agree with all my replies, but I do hope that they will help you reflect on your approaches to the work.

QUESTION: Do you wear a costume or play an instrument when you tell stories? How important are props with your stories?

ANSWER: I sometimes think people look a little disappointed when I tell them that I never wear a costume to tell stories, nor do I play an instrument. I seldom use any props. All of this strikes me as a bit too theatrical. Theatrical I am not, but dramatic, definitely yes.

Sometimes when telling a story I create the voices of the characters and employ the full range of emotions open to them. I'm not talking about getting in the way of the story by placing myself at the centre of things, but about letting the natural dramatic aspects of the story come to the surface.

Today, we tell stories in parks, around campfires, in public libraries, and in schools to children who have grown up with television and for whom close encounters with stories shared by interested adults are not the rule. Television has caused us to adopt different patterns of thinking about stories through rapid cuts, flashbacks, flash forwards, and commercial messages coming at rapid-fire pace. Attending to an oral tale requires getting used to if it's not been part of your life. For these reasons alone, if we are to establish communication with these listeners and capture their attention, we need the best dramatic readers and storytellers in the world. If that involves movement or vocal or body sound effects, then so be it! I repeat, however, that the dramatization must occur naturally, just as the voice we use should be that which is used in natural conversation, not one pitched an octave higher with a sing-song delivery.

QUESTION: Do you use the same voice style for every story?

ANSWER: Every story will demand a different vocal treatment. A story's needs should become apparent as you prepare it and consider what it means to you. Some stories will require an easy conversational tone; some, quiet, suspenseful telling; others, a mock-serious style. It is important to determine this and to make certain that you establish this mood authoritatively at the beginning of your tale.

You will find that in telling the story, you will make your most exciting discoveries. For example, a tiny creature who speaks in a deep voice might bring humor to a tense moment. A small detail described carefully can turn a seemingly harmless character into a dangerous one. The more opportunities you have to tell a story, the more this becomes apparent — volunteer to go into seniors' residences and day-care centres and tell stories around the family dinner table. I told one story for nearly a year before it began to feel right. Some stories take a while to understand.

Often, a story will require slightly different vocal interpretation depending on the age and experience of the listeners. Leila Berg, in *Folktales*, provides a useful comment: "There is one story here, Little Dog Turpie, that is loved unreservedly by all the children I tell it to, except one; and when I tell it to him, I have to tell it in a warm laughing way, that tells him that he and I are together on this, and we'll see the little old man and the little old woman and Little Dog Turpie safely through."

QUESTION: Do you ask questions after you tell a story?
ANSWER: No, I don't as a rule. If I am in a workshop setting with time to reflect on the tale I might encourage the listeners to tell each other about the story they beheld in their mind's eye as they listened. I do this to get young and old alike to appreciate the uniqueness of their own interpretation of a story and of those around them.

Usually children and adults tell me about images that stood out for them as they pictured the story, the ways they anticipated what was going to happen to the central character, stories they were reminded of as they listened, personal experiences from their own lives that came unbidden into their heads, personal feelings that they became aware of as the story unfolded, shapes or patterns of story that they perceived, and questions they had about incidents in the story or about the whole story in general. Often this is one of the areas where we enjoy the most fruitful discussions about a story. I find what people "retell" about their listening, imagining, and co-creating of the story far more exciting and insightful than any question I could ever think to ask. At the same time, everyone benefits by having their own perceptions of the story stretched by the ideas and comments of others in the group.

QUESTION: What are some of the greatest difficulties you face when storytelling?

ANSWER: I once shared a week of storytelling at Artpark with the great American storyteller, Brother Blue. Each day as we left the storytelling theatre, Blue would say: "Storytelling is hard work. It's plain hard work!"

Both outdoors and indoors it is indeed hard work. There are some things you can do however to make things easier on yourself. Setting appropriate physical conditions is one of them.

Outdoor storytelling is a great challenge. Shifting crowds and extraneous noise can be very disruptive. I have had to stop my story completely to accommodate jet aircraft, trucks, and police sirens, and once I was attacked by a dog who got excited about the story. When working outdoors, I try to look for a spot where movement behind me is reduced or screened and where I can practically stand in the crowd's lap. You must be clearly visible to everyone: I often hold my arms out at a forty-five degree angle from my body and request that no one sit outside the area bordered by my reach. Outdoors, you must be persistent and not appear annoyed. If interrupted, pause, then plunge right in again.

At the Hans Christian Andersen Storyhour in Central Park, New York, the storyteller stands at the base of the steps leading up to the statue of the beloved teller of tales. Usually, one or two monitors from the Hans Christian Andersen Storytelling Committee unobtrusively ensure that no one climbs onto the statue during the storytelling. Anyone, child or adult, who creates a disturbance or lights up any smoking material is given the cold, fishy eye or even a verbal reprimand. Telling a story on a summer Saturday morning in this great metropolitan park is an exceptional experience.

Telling stories indoors poses its own challenges. I have been in many schools and public libraries where finding the right place to tell takes some care.

Place yourself where you can be easily seen and where the lighting does not leave you in the shadows. Stand away from windows so that the listeners are not facing into the light. Similarly, look for a backdrop that isn't too busy (a display of bright paintings would distract). If it is necessary to stand to be seen, stand. If not, you might be more comfortable sitting down. Avoid standing or sitting behind a desk, lectern, or some other obstruction — it puts a barrier between you and your listeners. Once, in order to be seen in a university amphitheatre, I had to stand on a table. I don't recommend this, but do whatever is necessary to give yourself the best chance to communicate comfortably with your audience.

Consider acoustics whether indoors or out. Would you benefit from the use of a microphone? There is nothing more damaging than having to shout your story to be heard. The microphone can help you to save both your voice and your energy.

If you find yourself with no microphone and poor acoustics, try to bring your audience closer. In extreme circumstances I have done storytelling in the round to protect my voice. Physically, it's not an ideal way to tell a story, but in a difficult situation it can be a life saver.

QUESTION: Do you plan exactly what stories you will tell in a session and in what order they will be told?

ANSWER: If I am doing a specific program I plan meticulously what stories I will tell and I order them carefully. In addition, I list some back-up choices. All of this is written down on a piece of paper I keep in my pocket. However, this list is no indication of how the session will go.

Communicating with a group is exhilarating and creative. You, the storyteller, know your role, know what you're going to do, and know how you're going about it, but you can never tell how it is going to turn out. You must be prepared to be flexible — even if you have only one story — and handle whatever behavior the listeners throw up at you.

It's not unlike a football game where the quarterback calls the play and the team lines up. As the quarterback approaches the centre, he scans the opposing defence. If he anticipates that the defence has read the play, he quickly calls "an audible" and the team prepares to go with the new plan. So it is with storytelling. You face the group, glance around at the listeners, take note of body language, signs of restlessness, and overall mood, and try to read the situation. Often in that split second before I open my mouth to speak, I have made the decision to abandon the story I wanted to tell and chosen another.

QUESTION: Could you be more specific about what would cause you to change your mind about telling a story and what you would do about it?

66

ANSWER: If I have a group deliberately sitting as far from me as possible and who ignore my invitation to move forward, I will try to jolly them along a bit. One of my favorite ploys with a group like this is to use a lot of rhetorical questions in order to build an awareness of how the story is unfolding, to encourage anticipation and to focus the listening. (For example: Have you ever met anyone like this? How do you think you would feel at this point?) Taking this ploy is very risky however, for if you don't work deep within the context of the story you can quickly lose control. If you can employ such a device to get the crowd with you, though, that's great.

I have worked with groups where settling in has been an issue. Sometimes it takes two or three stories just to calm them until they give themselves over to a tale.

Another device I will use to focus a group is to select a story that calls upon the audience to chant a refrain or sing a chorus. With an especially restless group, such a strategy gives the storyteller badly needed breaks in order to compose himself or herself. It also provides an opportunity to observe the group carefully and adjust the telling as necessary.

QUESTION: What do you consider to be one of the most important assets a storyteller, working in a public sense, can have?

ANSWER: Energy! You must throw yourself wholeheartedly into the work. Live it. Your audience must feel the enjoyment you are getting from the work. Even when you are feeling exhausted you must not show it. Your desire to tell a story, as well as your confidence in your own preparation and ability to tell the story, goes a long way in helping you to summon that energy.

The energy of the audience is important too. A lethargic, unresponsive group can leave you dragging. A keen, responsive group that hangs on to every word and practically breathes in unison can buoy you up and even invigorate you.

With a difficult group, I establish my foundation of support pretty quickly. I look for the shining eyes and the glowing countenances of the individuals who are with me. There is always one, usually more than one. Although I maintain strong eye contact with the whole group and try even harder to carry the story to them, my eyes flick regularly back and forth to those supporters who are helping to carry me.

QUESTION: How do you deal with interruptions to the story?

ANSWER: If you mean interruption as in a listener speaking out, usually to ask a question, I answer directly by incorporating that question and my answer into the context of the story. For example: "You ask why the boy allowed himself to be caught by the giant? He's under a very powerful spell, do you remember? And so powerful was that spell. . . ." And so on.

Once, in a park, a drunk wandered into a storytelling session. He stood, swaying gently, trying to figure out what was going on. His presence was creating tension in the audience. Then he did what everyone was afraid he would do. He shouted out a comment over top of my voice. I kept going. He shouted again. The group was becoming quite agitated. Before anything else could happen I replied directly to him, not skipping a moment of the story. He nodded and kept quiet for the rest of the story, then he shambled off.

Even the keenest listener can be lost to an unanticipated interruption. Often, everything you have built in terms of a story can be blown up in front of you and there's little you can do about it. One time I was telling a story to a large group of teachers in a school gym. I was approaching the climax of the story when, suddenly, a voice boomed over the public address system with a list of licence numbers for illegally parked cars. I couldn't believe what happened next. People leapt to their feet, chairs scraped and banged, and high heels clicked across the wooden floors. When the confusion died, I quickly resumed the story and mustering all the confidence that I could, I finished it. In that kind of situation all you can do is keep your composure and finish the telling in the most dignified manner possible.

Sometimes the storyteller can be the source of interruption. Surrounding the story with too much idle chat or breaking the story flow to indulge in moralizing or long-winded explanations will mar the listener's story experience. Keep introductory remarks to a minimum and start right in with your story, telling it in close logical sequence in a conversational tone of voice which portrays with clarity and authority the events and emotions contained in the tale.

QUESTION: How does the classroom teacher build and maintain a repertoire of stories when the opportunity to tell any given story occurs about once a year?

ANSWER: First of all, many children enjoy hearing a favorite story told over and over. A few great stories can serve you rather well. Now having said that, yes, building a repertoire might appear daunting to a busy individual. There are several possibilities to help.

Patterned stories, such as cumulative tales, are quickly learned. Once you recognize the pattern, the problem, characters, and situations are easy to absorb. As you explore patterned tales with your students in their writing, more ideas will emerge.

Tale types such as trickster tales, tales about foolish people, and tales of wisdom share common motifs, common themes. As you become familiar with these and with all the variants of a specific tale, you suddenly realize that it's possible to know a lot of stories in a short time. For example most Cinderella stories have a character of privilege brought low who must reach up and conquer adversity. You know how the story has to work; now you need to furnish the details. In a book such as *The Cinderella Story* by Neil Philip you could find three or four variants of the story and learn them all at once.

I would also advise keeping a journal on what works best with your students. Doing this will help you build some surefire hits and provide clues for the kinds of stories you might collect. Some random jottings from my many journals follow.

Sample Journal Entries

Journal entry — A Fall Fair
The space is noisy; the crowd constantly coming and going. Adults bring children close to the storyteller then retreat and hang back on the fringes. Recommend use of a microphone next year. Stories don't work here without it. Also do more to encourage parents to sit with their children.

Journal entry — *The Spider's Palace* (Hughes)
Finding the right voice for this story is important. Opening can be a bit scary. Try for an offhand or matter-of-fact tone.

Journal entry — *I Can Squash Elephants* (Carrick)
Revise the ending. At the moment it seems anti-climactic. Bring story to an end after "frog's" closing speech.

Journal entry — A Christmas Program
All stories were very powerful. Audience was very quiet and reflective at

conclusion. Give listeners more time to "come back" with such material before going on to the next story.

Journal entry — Opening Day — Artpark Summer of '81
Today's session had to be the hardest ever. The audience consisted of sixty preschoolers, a summer day camp for preteens, several families, a dog and a bus load of "seniors" — all eating box lunches. A garbage truck smashed bottles for the first fifteen minutes over at the theater and a training jet made six thundering passes. A steady, rapid delivery saved the day along with lots of participation work.

QUESTION: What should beginning storytellers look for to improve their style?

ANSWER: I am convinced that storytelling is an art form which can be practised by anyone who has the desire.

I have watched professional storytellers tell stories that, like so many TV situation comedies, carry no weight. They have performed in a slick polished style that has brought a crowd to its feet applauding.

I have also watched beginners tell a story in a halting fashion with such conviction that it has reached deep into the hearts and minds of the listeners and left them feeling complete satisfaction.

Two things are basic to good storytelling, at least as far as I am concerned: choosing a story that will help the listener to understand the richness of life and the complexities of being human, and telling it with sincerity. Of course delivery is important, but having faith in your material and demonstrating it are essential.

Many beginners tend to rush through their material so be aware of this. Try to begin slowly and make the most of every word and every sound. Clarity of speech is important.

Another skill to develop is the use of silence. The pause is an excellent device to help build suspense and to permit your listeners to savor the pleasures of anticipation. I cannot give you foolproof guidelines for its use, but I can encourage you to let your story work for you. Where are the suspenseful bits, which will benefit from slow build-up with pauses injected at critical points? Which passages should be skipped over quickly and where should you go slowly? In most instances, careful reading of the material will furnish you with clues.

Decide too what element or elements are important to your tale. Sometimes beginning tellers don't consider this and give equal weight to everything in the story. There's an Eleanor Farjeon story, "The Lovebirds," that I like very much. The element I like to highlight is the overriding mood of the tale and I work with that mood when I tell the tale. In another story, setting may matter most, especially if we are entering an unfamiliar world.

QUESTION: I worry that my vocabulary isn't good enough for telling a story without the book in front of me. What can I do to overcome this?

ANSWER: I think that if you can relax, make the most of the words you have, enjoy them, and make everything happen as you say them, then there is little to be concerned about. As you learn more stories you soon discover that many expressions and word patterns will transfer almost automatically from one story to the next.

QUESTION: When you encounter difficult, foreign, or obsolete words in folktales, do you substitute for them when working with young children?

ANSWER: I don't ever substitute for the words of a story. They are part of the story and its style and unless they interfere directly with meaning, I offer no explanations. Quite frequently, hearing a word used within the context of the story will suffice to make its meanings understood. I am convinced that words not understood have a charm and magic of their own which children enjoy. I find it exciting to puzzle and ponder over strange words, to listen to their sound, and to guess at their sense.

If I think a word is going to block significant meaning, I simply explain it within the context of the story without interrupting the flow. Often young children will ask in the middle of a story for explanation of a word. Without any fuss I tell them and the story remains unbroken.

QUESTION: How important are the voices in a story? Do you have to characterize vocally in order to tell the story well?

ANSWER: Here again, you must do what comes naturally to you. I never deliberately set out to do voice characterizations, yet my inner ear continually guides me on this. I have heard storytellers set out to characterize then lose track of which voice sounds like what. Your awareness of the emotions and thoughts of a character at any given time in the story are probably a better approach to characterization than being concerned about the sound.

QUESTION: I can't do dialects very well. What would you advise?

ANSWER: I can't do them either, so I don't try. Tell the story in a manner comfortable to you. There's little worse than listening to someone attempt dialects and not pull them off.

QUESTION: My voice isn't particularly interesting to listen to. Do you have any tips?

ANSWER: The voice we have is the voice we must use. A common voice problem concerns breathing. Much strain occurs to the throat if breathing is shallow. Learning to breathe deeply and making sure you have sufficient air greatly relieve tension both in the throat and neck.

It's really important to warm up your voice before telling a story. That warm-up needn't be elaborate either. I find humming very helpful. You can hum familiar tunes varying the pitch, rate, and volume. Ten to fifteen minutes of this will help get your voice ready. Also try breathing in to a count of eight and exhaling to a count of eight.

Remember to release the tension from the rest of your body too. I do a bit of stretching (leaning against a wall and sliding down is my favorite) and brisk walking about, swinging my arms freely.

Being relaxed and confident about your story and enjoying the sounds of the words improve vocal quality. Have fun experimenting with the story too. Where should passages be delivered slowly? Where might a change in volume add to the overall texture of the telling?

It's also important to listen to other people tell stories and to note what they do with their voices. Listening to taped stories is also good; however, when it comes to working the voice in audience situations, I find I like to watch other tellers to get the big picture.

QUESTION: How do you involve listeners in the story?

ANSWER: I involve listeners in the story in three ways (not all at once, necessarily). The simplest, most natural way is to invite everyone to chime in with you on repetitions, refrains, chants, or songs. Children will do this naturally with stories they love to hear again and again. If there is already a little sound motif in the story, listeners can be easily persuaded to help you handle it.

Sometimes I will ask an audience to help me heighten the suspense of a fun story by providing sound effects. Before telling the story, I catalogue the sounds we need. For example, we might need the sound of wind on a stormy night or the creaking of a shutter on rusty hinges or raindrops on a tin roof. Once we have agreed upon and rehearsed the sounds, I tell the story. The listeners have to be alert for the clues in the story that indicate when specific sounds are required. This activity is especially good for focusing a group that needs to release energy.

The third way I involve listeners is to give out roles. These can be formal roles in a story where one or two characters repeat a line or expression again and again. Once the audience understands how the story is working and who speaks when, all you have to do is point and pause and they usually respond. For example in "Burnie's Hill" cited earlier, I give the answer to the questions posed by the group.

There are also opportunities for informal roles, often in crowd scenes where individual comments can be ad-libbed by the listeners on cue from the storyteller. For example: "I understand that the step-mother and the stepsister made Little Sister do all the work inside the house and all the work outside the house. I'll bet you neighbors know what some of those tasks were. . . ."

QUESTION: What new ideas do you have for us to develop our own stories?

ANSWER: Probably the simplest stories you can tell are ones about your own childhood. They may be centred on holiday celebrations, special friends, your most embarrassing moment, your first ride on a rollercoaster, a kindness done to you, the scariest person you ever met, relationships with other members of the family. Children like to hear stories about the lives of their parents or teachers when they were little. Photographs make wonderful prompts here.

Russell Hoban's book, *La Corona and the Tin Frog*, reminded me that a child's toys can become the subject matter for invented stories. I keep a small box filled with unusual little wind-up toys that I find on my travels. At the moment, the box contains an orange crocodile whose jaws open and close once it is wound, a green frog with a baby frog riding piggy-back behind, and a little yellow happy face creature, also a wind-up. They are a wonderful group to build stories around.

A well-known story such as "The Three Bears" can also be set in the familiar environs of your own neighborhood: the local convenience store, the park, and so on. Local figures, the neighborhood cat, and the children themselves can be woven into the tale.

Nursery rhymes can launch story making. Some nursery rhymes are sufficiently open-ended to permit extensions of the tale. Others adapt nicely to the creation of additional verses. For example, "On Saturday night I lost my wife" could be extended to what happened on Sunday night, Monday night, Tuesday night, and so on.

FEATURE ON WORD MUSIC COMPOSITIONS

Another method of creating stories focuses on the sounds and rhythms of words hooked together thematically. I call this vocal jazz. Vocal jazz celebrates words — words that began as sounds as well as the sounds words contain and the pattern of sounds words make when strung together. Patterns can be made using words from many sources. A word music composition on the world of soup might begin with the assembling of a soup's ingredients, include the chanting of unusual soup recipes (Alibaba Noodle Cream, Cold Creme Curry), and end with the final slurp of a satisfied soup eater.

A. The following word music composition was built up around the idea of talk.

First, synonyms for the word *talk* were brainstormed. The list contained such words as *blabber, blither, drone, yammer, bellow, chat, jabber, prattle, announce, exclaim, quibble, gossip, yap, declaim, drawl, expound.*

Next, categories of talk were considered. Beyond the example of the film title *Pillow Talk* come bus talk, gutter talk, staffroom talk, locker room talk, street talk, double talk, hand talk, baby talk, back talk, shop talk, big talk, in-talk, bilateral talk, beans talk (a small pun), over-the-backfence talk, behind-closed-doors-talk, and under-the-table talk.

According to the context in which talk occurs there is vocabulary to describe it. For example, we could have innuendo, scolding, monologue, dialogue, parley, lecture, sermon, eulogy, debate, soliloquy, interview, forum, diatribe, quarrel, *tête-à-tête,* proposition, jamboree, *coroboree* (Australian), *chautauqua* (Native American).

To conclude, expressions used to stop talk were reviewed. These included "pipe down," "silence," "hold your tongue," "knock it off," "quiet," "ssh!," "cool it," "seal your lips," "stuff it," "clam up," "stifle yourself," "stow the gab," "*fermez la bouche,*" "shush yourself," "put a plug in it," "on hold."

From all the raw material gathered, the development of the jazz composition evolved. Mainly, the effects desired were interesting sounds and patterns of sounds. Here is one example of a communal composition.

ALL:	TALK!	(followed by a babbling of voices lasting about ten seconds)
ALL:	TALK!	
SOLO 1:	Bellow	
SOLO 2:	Yap	(to be spoken
SOLO 3:	Jabber	in cheerleader
SOLO 4:	Yammer	fashion)

Note:
The instruction here had been to select four words from the first list and arrange them in an interesting sound pattern.

ALL:	bellow, yap, jabber, yammer	
SOLO 5:	Chat	
SOLO 6:	Prattle	
SOLO 7:	Blither	
SOLO 8:	Blather	
ALL:	chat, prattle, blither, blather	*Note*: This sequence
GROUP A:	(chant) shop talk, shop talk *etc*.	was built up
GROUP B:	(chant) double talk, double talk *etc*.	cumulatively, by
GROUP C:	(chant) over-the-backfence talk *etc*.	adding groups
GROUP D:	(chant) under-the-table talk *etc*.	one, two, three, and four, one at a
ALL:	Chautauqua, soliloquy, innuendo	time.
	Chautauqua, soliloquy, innuendo	
	Chautauqua, soliloquy, innuendo	
	(chorus continues but fades under as solos are called over)	
SOLO 9:	*Fermez la bouche!*	

SOLO 10:   Hold your tongue!
SOLO 11:   Stifle yourself!
SOLO 12:   Knock it off!
ALL: CUT!

Many old storytelling techniques were used to bring our vocal jazz piece to life. These included call and response (echo), chiming-in, and competitive chanting. In addition, the experience included word building, word association, gaming with words, playing with synonyms, homonyms, and antonyms, and experimentation with onomatopoeia.

Choosing a concept, teasing it out into its constituent parts, then designing a simple framework on which to hang the words is what it's all about. The activity is easily adapted to all ages and serves as a vehicle for speaking aloud with expression, with ease, and with joy.

Browse through concept books such as *Boats* and *Rain* by Donald Crewes or Ted Harrison's *Northern Alphabet* for additional ideas for word music compositions.

B. Here is a composition that was developed from a nursery rhyme. I have often used this in storytelling workshops to review story patterns from the oral tradition as well as to help the members of a group to recall story experiences from their own folk heritage.

GROUP A: I'll tell you a story about Jackanory
(chants   And now my story's begun.
twice)   I'll tell you another about
            Jack and his brother
            And now my story is done
GROUP B: (begin when group A reaches "begun")
(chants   I'll tell you a story about Jackanory
twice)   And now my story's begun.
            I'll tell you another about
            Jack and his brother
            And now my story is done
GROUP A: Again and Again
(chant)   Again and Again
            Again and Again
            (fade and down)

GROUP B: In a dark dark house
(chant)   There's a dark dark stair
          Down the dark dark stair
          There's a dark dark cellar
          Down the dark dark cellar
          There's a dark dark box
          In the dark dark box
          There's a Ghost!
SOLO 1:   SCREAM!
GROUP B: On and on, on and on
(chant)   On and on, on and on
          (fade and down)
GROUP A: Pete and Repete sat on a fence
(chant)   Pete fell off
          Who was left?
GROUP B: REPETE!
GROUP A: Pete and Repete sat on a fence
          Pete fell off
          (fade and down)
GROUP B: BACK AND FORTH
          BACK AND FORTH
          BACK AND FORTH
GROUP A: What's your name?
GROUP B: Mary Jane
GROUP A: Where do you live?
GROUP B: Cabbage Lane
GROUP A: What's your number?
GROUP B: Bread and cucumber!
GROUP A: The grand old Duke of York
(singing) He had ten thousand men
          He marched them up to the top of a hill
          And marched them down again
          (keep repeating)
GROUP B: London Bridge is falling down, falling down
(singing) *etc*.
GROUP A: (fade out Grand Old Duke of York and chant softly and
          increase volume)
          And now my story is done

And now my story is done

GROUP B: (fade out London Bridge and chant softly and increase volume)

And now my story is done

And now my story is done

ALL: And now my story is DONE!

In the end, the work featured infinity stories (Pete and Repete); stories with repetitive sequences (In a dark, dark house); question and answer structures which are found in many old ballads, folk songs, and playground lore; and stories sung in varying movement patterns (London Bridge — arch, Grand Old Duke — advancing/retreating lines). Many more stories were recalled, and told. We couldn't work them all in. Some rhymes and stories were told in languages other than English. These gave many ideas for using varying textures of sound.

QUESTION: How do you integrate music, movement, and drama into storytelling?

ANSWER: The vocal jazz demonstrated in the previous example is one way to explore sound and rhythm and song. There is also potential for movement.

Another interesting approach is to work with traditional singing and drama games. All of us have participated naturally in such drama games as London Bridge Is Falling Down, Ring-a-Ring-o'-Roses and Old Roger Is Dead and Laid in His Grave. One of the best books on the subject I know is *Step It Down* by Bessie Jones and Bessie Lomax Hawes. Here are wonderful stories in dance, mime, drama, and song. Music notation is provided, but for those who learn best by ear there is a companion tape.

Children's Games in Street and Playground by Iona and Peter Opie is also another excellent source of this kind of material. (Examples of singing and drama games are featured in chapter 8.)

QUESTION: What type of stories do young children enjoy hearing best?

ANSWER: In her book *The Ordinary and the Fabulous,* Elizabeth Cook says:

Stories that lead to doing things are all the more attractive to children who are active rather than passive creatures. Myths and fairytales provide an unusually abundant choice of things to do. Largely because they are archetypal and anonymous (in quality, if not in provenance), they will stand reinterpretation in many forms without losing their character. They can be recreated by children not only in words but in drama, in mime, in dance and in painting. Action in them is not fussy, and lends itself to qualitative expression in the movements of the human body and in the shapes and colors of non-figurative painting.

I can think of no better answer.

FIVE

Reading Stories to Children

Matt decided to skip B for bone. In the night he had thought of a better way.

"This book isn't a treaty," he began. "It's a story. It's about a man who gets shipwrecked on a desert island. I'll read some of it out loud to show you."

He opened Robinson Crusoe *at the first page and began to read.*

I was born in the year 1632,

in the city of York. . . .

He stopped. He remembered suddenly how the first time he had tried to read this book he had found that first page so dull he had come close to giving up right there. He had better skip the beginning and get on with the story if he wanted to catch Attean's attention.

"I'll read the part about the storm at sea," he said.

He had read the book so many times that he knew exactly where to find the right page. Taking a deep breath, as though he were struggling in the water himself, he chose the page where Robinson Crusoe was dashed from the lifeboat and swallowed up in the sea.

Nothing can describe the confusion of thought which I felt when I sunk into the water, for though I swam very well, yet I could not deliver myself from the waves so as to draw breath . . . for I saw the sea come after me as high as a great bill, and as furious as an enemy. . . .

From *The Sign of the Beaver,* by Elizabeth George Speare

I once received a letter dictated by a group of Kindergarten children to their teacher thanking me for visiting and telling stories. Included in the letter was this line, "When you said the words that helped us think the pictures."

Children continue to remind me that listening to stories is important because it gives them an opportunity to think in the story world.

Helping Children "Think the Pictures"

I am convinced that the mechanical challenges of silent reading prevent scores of children from living in and through the life of a story as it unfolds.

When the children listen to a story, however, the mechanical difficulties of reading are put aside and the storyteller's pacing, intonation, gestures, and expression support their efforts to "think the pictures." (It goes without saying that the quality of the story matters greatly. Poor stories do not create such opportunities for the imagination.)

A successful listener needs to be a storyteller too. Far from being passive, the listener is actively participating in the re-creation of that story. And this reality becomes an important reason for presenting stories out loud to children; the listening experience helps them to comprehend the role they are expected to play in the story game. This role will be the same when they read for themselves. Author Katherine Paterson describes it:

> My aim is to engage young readers in the life of a story which came out of me but which is not mine, but ours. I don't just want a young reader's time or attention, I want his life. I want his senses, his imagination, his intellect, his emotions and all the experiences he has known breathing life into the words upon the page. It doesn't matter how high my aim or how polished my craft, I know that without the efforts of my reader, I have accomplished nothing. The answer to the old puzzle about the tree falling in the unpopulated wilderness is that it makes no noise. I have not written a book for children unless the book is brought to life by the child who reads it. It is a co-operative venture. My aim is to do my part so well that the young reader will delight to join me as co-author.

When we read or tell a story our aim is identical to that described by Katherine Paterson: to invite our listeners to join us as co-tellers.

Another reason we read to children is to extend their reading range and strengthen their ability to take in complex language. Children's capacity to take in language is generally ahead of their ability to read;

even so it will be necessary to pass over some unimportant details, shorten lengthy passages of description or asides, and perhaps tell some segments in our own words.

Get Past the Words

When you read aloud, there is a physical object, the book, to contend with as well as language constructions. The level of sophistication of the printed word will also demand keen listening on the part of your audience. Anyone who picks up a book to read aloud without some preparation runs the risk of wallowing into an experience which will be no joy for either reader or listener.

Like the storyteller who works from memory, the reader of stories must also bring thoughts, feelings, characters, and ideas to life. The reader of stories must also be able to visualize what is happening and transmit this to the listener.

When reading aloud, the task is so much more than speaking print. Knowing when to turn the page of a picture book in order to build suspense or keep pace with the flow of the text can make an enormous difference. And even the best story can benefit from a little pruning in a read-aloud situation, as Matt demonstrates in the opening quote.

Practising the story out loud will also help reveal the qualities of sound and rhythm it possesses and give some indication of the places to pause in a way that the eye can't detect. At the same time you can consider the vocal treatment to be used. Should delivery be matter-of-fact? Would some voice characterization add more life? Aim to vary the range of your voice, which can be seen as a musical instrument. Unless you're after a specific effect, speaking in a monotone is something to avoid.

Determine the overall mood of the material and establish that mood at the outset. If you are dealing with a selection that releases strong emotions in you, go over and over the work in order to distance yourself a bit from the emotional part. Your feelings will register with your listeners even though you are maintaining control.

Study the structure of the piece too in order to determine where care (possibly slowing down) should be exercised in revealing important clues that will have an impact on the ending. You want to keep your listeners anticipating.

I like to indicate on my text, with a pencil if appropriate or with Post-it notes, where I am stopping and starting and what I am deleting. Try to keep your marking simple. Too much detail can often create confusion for you rather than clarity.

Choice of material can contribute greatly to the ease of your success in reading aloud. Just as much of the appeal of folktale lies in its ability to capture interest quickly, look for stories to read aloud that readily engage the listener. Plunge the listener into an action-packed situation. Notice how quickly we are pulled into the events of Philippa Pearce's *The Battle of Bubble and Squeak*.

> The middle of the night, and everyone in the house asleep.
>
> Everyone? Then what was that noise?
>
> Creak! and then, after a pause, Creak! And then, Creak!
>
> And then, Creak! As regular as clockwork — but was this just clockwork? Behind the creaking, the lesser sound of some delicate tool working on metal.
>
> The girls heard nothing. Amy Parker was so young that nothing ever disturbed her sleep. Peggy, too, slept normally.
>
> Sid Parker, their brother, heard in his dreams. He was the eldest by a little, and slept more lightly. Besides, he had been half expecting to hear something. He had dreaded to hear it. He came swimming up from the depths of his dreams to the surface: now he was wide awake, listening. Creak! he heard; and then Creak! . . . Creak! . . . Creak! Sid broke into a sweat as he listened. And their mother? Mrs. Sparrow heard it. The noise woke her, as the crying of her children would have woken her. But this was someone else's job. She nudged her husband, the children's stepfather. She nudged and nudged until Bill Sparrow stirred, groaned. He had been dreaming of the garden: mostly marrows, and runner beans that towered over their apple tree . . . "Bill!" she whispered. "Come on! Wake up!" "Yes," he said. "Just a minute, and I'll do that." "Listen!" Creak! and then, Creak! And then, Creak! "Can't you hear it?" "Yes." "What is it?" "I don't know." "But it's in the house!" "Yes it is." "Downstairs!" "Yes." "Bill, what are you going to do about it?"

The brisk, suspense-filled dialogue, the short sentences, and the vivid images catch us up, don't they? "What happens next?" has been deftly established. Not all stories hook the listener this quickly. Some lively dramatic reading on the part of the reader might be necessary for several chapters until the story takes hold. In a one-on-one situation this is often less difficult than when trying to read to a group. In group situations especially, the time spent in getting prepared to read will pay off.

The actual read-aloud should commence slowly, then quicken as it becomes apparent that the listeners have slipped into the story world. I find that beginning with a slow pace helps the voice to carry and makes it easy to switch to dialogue or build tension.

It is important to look up from the book frequently and to note the signals that the listeners are sending. A furrowed brow, an indifferent expression, or restlessness might mean your style or the material requires attention. Be sure to make direct eye contact with your listeners periodically. Also, look for special phrases that you might want to highlight by meeting your listeners' eyes.

I try to make my characters larger than life. If you can, change voices for the characters. Above all don't hesitate to be a bit playful with your voice. Gestures are fine too if they suit the moment.

Choosing a Read-Aloud Story

As suggested earlier, some books read aloud better than others. Haunt your local public library and school library. Talk to librarians, other parents, teachers, and children in order to discover what they have enjoyed. These titles have worked especially well for many:

- *Mr. Gumpy's Outing,* by John Burningham
  A delightful cumulative tale with lots of repetition for young listeners to become involved in. A great favorite with young children.

- *Funnybones,* by Janet and Allan Ahlberg
  A simple repetitive story pattern becomes the vehicle for the hilarious nighttime adventures of two Mutt-and-Jeff–type skeletons. A wonderful book for out loud performance. There are singing bits too.

- *Where the Wild Things Are*, by Maurice Sendak
  The story of Max and his adventure with the Wild Things who "roared their terrible roars and gnashed their terrible teeth" has

become a modern children's classic. Don't overlook Sendak's *In the Night Kitchen* or *Outside Over There*.

- *Mr. Rabbit and the Lovely Present*, by Charlotte Zolotow
A little girl wants to give her mother a birthday present but can't think of something. With the help of an imaginary rabbit friend she explores the possibilities. The play on words and ideas is thoroughly entertaining. Another contemporary classic with stunning pictures by Maurice Sendak.

- *Frog and Toad Are Friends,* by Arnold Lobel
The Frog and Toad series is produced in an "I Can Read Format" but this title, as well as *Frog and Toad Together* and *Frog and Toad All Year,* is so entertaining that it makes a wonderful read-aloud. One of my favorites in this collection is "The Story."

- *Lilly's Purple Plastic Purse*, by Kevin Henkes
Lilly is infatuated with her teacher until she is disciplined by him. Then she seeks revenge. This funny, touching story reaches into the hearts and minds of young children and the child in all of us.

- *Jack and the Beanstalk*, by Alan Garner
The lively language practically leaps off the page in this outstanding retelling of the famous English folktale. All read-alouds should be this much fun.

- *Rainbow Crow,* by Nancy Van Laan
Nancy Van Laan's retelling of this beautiful Lenape legend is skillfully crafted for reading aloud. Beatriz Vidal's lovely water color illustrations are an added bonus.

- *The Amazing Bone*, by William Steig
William Steig's main characters often undergo fantastic transformations, which trigger a cliffhanger adventure. In this story Pearl Pig finds a talking bone and the action erupts. (See also *Dr. DeSoto).*

- *How Tom Beat Captain Najork and His Hired Sportsmen*, by Russell Hoban
Aunt Fidget Wonkham Strong wore an iron hat and took no nonsense from anyone. Her practical joker nephew, Tom, fooled around too much and needed to be taught a lesson. Captain Najork

is called in to straighten out the unruly lad. Tom's fooling around pays off handsomely as he squares off with Najork.

- *Josepha*, by Jim McGugan
  Here is a touching story of an immigrant boy struggling to find his place in the Canadian West at the end of the nineteenth century. Strong illustrations by Murray Kimber help to emphasize the strangeness and isolation felt by Josepha.

- *The Wild Boy*, by Mordicai Gerstein
  Gerstein tells the true story of the wild child of Aveyron who was captured in southern France in 1800 and of the young doctor, Jean-Marc-Gaspard Itard, who worked with him for several years.

- *Wilma Unlimited*, by Kathleen Krull
  This true story about an Olympic athlete and triple gold medal winner captures magnificently Wilma Rudolph's battle to overcome polio and her tremendous will to succeed. *Wilma Unlimited* is a visually stunning book as well thanks to the illustrations by David Diaz.

- *Sarah and the People of Sand River*, by W. D. Valgardson
  Sarah lives with her father on the shores of Lake Winnipeg but because she speaks only Icelandic she is placed with a family in Winnipeg to learn English. The family turns on her and Sarah must try to get back home during a freezing cold winter. Set at the end of the nineteenth century, the story is a fascinating blend of true events and fantasy.

Other excellent read-aloud books not to be missed:

The True Story of the 3 Little Pigs, by Jon Scieszka
Bone Button Borscht, by Aubrey Davis
"The Porcelain Man," by Richard Kennedy, in *Richard Kennedy: Collected Stories*
3 Billy Goats Gruff . . . or 3 Strikes Yer Out!, by Ted Dewan
The Village of Round and Square Houses, by Ann Grifalconi
The Moon's Revenge, by Joan Aiken
The Mousehole Cat, by Antonia Barber
The Pirate Who Tried to Capture the Moon, by Dennis Haseley
Amazing Grace, by Mary Hoffman

My Rows and Piles of Corns, by Tolalwa Mollel
Red Parka Mary, by Peter Eyvindson
Jeremiah Learns to Read, by Jo Ellen Bogart
Weslandia, by Paul Fleischman
The Dragon's Pearl, by Julie Lawson
Once Upon a Golden Apple, by Jean Little and Maggie de Vries

Types of Read-Aloud Opportunities

In read-aloud situations, adults are often amazed at children's ability to fill in, word for word, parts of a well-loved tale or to correct an errant reader who has omitted a favorite scene or sentence.

Children are usually willing partners in the telling of a story. Not only is the experience pleasurable for them, but it is an opportunity to enhance listening, speaking, and language awareness. As the children wait for their part, not only are listening skills increased, but the children's sense of what constitutes a story is sharpened.

An important skill for becoming an independent reader is anticipation. The suggestions that follow encourage both anticipation and participation. If children are to become lifelong readers, enjoyment of stories and response to stories is a must.

Single-sitting Books

Picture books, folk and fairy tales, and short stories can generally be read in a single session and still permit time for talk on the story. There should also be a chance to study the illustrations and do some co-operative reading aloud.

Many stories of these kinds contain a repeated phrase, simple pattern of dialogue or refrain, which children will chant spontaneously. Once children are familiar with the way the story is working, the reader can pause in anticipation of the phrase, verse, question, or answer and let them *chime in.* The formula tales listed in chapter 2 all encourage listener participation. Also look for these titles:

All Join In, by Quentin Blake
The Elephant and the Bad Baby, by Elfrida Vipont
The Park in the Dark, by Martin Waddell

Yummers, by James Marshall
Millions of Cats, by Wanda Gag

The following stories all contain much repetition. They are easily followed by children as the established bits are repeated again and again.

Hairy Maclary Scattercat, by Lynley Dodd
The Wheels on the Bus, by Maryann Kovalski
Clay Boy, by Mirra Ginsburg
We're Going on a Bear Hunt, by Michael Rosen
Joseph Had a Little Overcoat, by Simms Taback
Amazing Anthony Ant, by Lorna and Graham Philpot

Some stories feature extensive dialogue between two characters. Once children are familiar with the material, roles can be taken and the story read co-operatively. For example, in Eric Carle's *The Grouchy Ladybug,* a belligerent ladybug tries to pick a series of fights with all manner of creatures. In each case, the ladybug addresses her adversaries with the words:

Want to fight?/Oh you're not big enough.

The child can take the ladybug's repetitive speech while the adult reader handles narration and the direct responses of the various creatures.

> **At seven o'clock it saw a stag beetle.**
> **"Hey you," said the grouchy ladybug: "Want to fight?"**
> **"If you insist," said the stag beetle, opening its jaws.**
> **"Oh you're not big enough," said the grouchy ladybug and flew off.**

As you proceed, page size and typography change with each encounter. How this will be accommodated in the oral interpretation is the fun of the experience.

Another good source for this kind of experience is *A Flea Story* by Leo Lionni. This little fantasy is a kind of two-character play starring an adventurous flea who wants to step out and see the world and the flea's pal who is somewhat of a "stick-in-the-mud." The fleas embark on an adventure, viewed as exciting by one and as vexing by the other.

The direct speech of each insect is enclosed in a boldly outlined balloon. Each outline is a different color. After one or two practice runs, child and adult can engage in some lively dramatic oral reading. How will the colors of the balloon borders be incorporated into your interpretation?

Here are a few additional titles that might also be explored:

Yo! Yes?, by Chris Raschka
Red Is Best, by Kathy Stinson
Hush!: A Thai Lullaby, by Minfong Ho
Peace at Last, by Jill Murphy
Everyone Asked about You, by Theodore Faro Gross

A similar kind of pairs reading can be explored with question and answer stories, Karla Kuskin's *Roar and More* being a good example. Each double spread in this old favorite contains a verse about an animal on the left-hand side and a picture of the creature on the right-hand side. For example, on the left of the first spread we are told:

> If a lion comes to visit
> Don't open your door
> Just firmly ask "What is it?"
> And listen to him roar.

On the right side of the spread is a picture of the "jungle king" himself. When the page turns, however, the entire second spread is filled with the word R O A R in bold black lettering.

The reader can handle the text and the listener can respond to the word and picture clues by supplying the appropriate sound when the page is turned; this provides a simply delightful shared reading experience for a young child and adult reader.

Other books that offer this kind of opportunity include

Have You Seen My Duckling?, by Nancy Tafuri
Hattie and the Fox, by Mem Fox
Where's Spot?, by Eric Hill
Would You Rather?, by John Burningham

Excerpts from Longer Works

Often I find myself in situations where I will be reading to a group one time only. If I am trying to interest listeners in reading a selection for themselves, I will sometimes select a series of key passages from a book, which focus on one story theme or character. In this book, for example, I have featured excerpts from *The Voyage of QV66* that comment on the nature and art of storytelling and reading aloud. Taken together, they provide an interesting strand which runs through that novel. By choosing related passages, I also gain more opportunities to provide a rewarding listening experience.

If identifying linked passages seems too difficult, try to lift segments from longer works which stand on their own as stories even though they are lacking their context. You might look for the following examples:

"Tricky Bear," pages 131–39, *The Man in the Ceiling,* by Jules Feiffer (HarperCollins)

"What a Great Day!," pages 136–40, *The Wheel on the School,* by Meindert Dejong (Harper & Row)

"The Cat," pages 29–39, *The Daydreamer,* by Ian McEwan (Knopf)

"East of the Sun, West of the Moon," pages 43–65, *Head and Tales,* Susan Price (Faber & Faber)

"Hello Bluebird," pages 40–43, *That Scatterbrain Booky,* by Bernice Thurman Hunter (Scholastic)

Serialization

Reading a chapter a day until the book is finished is a common way of handling longer works. If there is any drawback to this approach it is that the reading can stretch on too long, causing significant details of the story to be lost. Where considerable time elapses between readings, serialization might be a poor choice.

There are, however, many books that adapt well to this approach. Undoubtedly one of the best is *The Iron Man* by Ted Hughes. Each of the five chapters can be read in about forty minutes, permitting the book to be completed in a week. It is, of course, possible to condense the reading time of a longer work by combining the reading with some narrating in your own words.

We owe it to our children to select books that will stretch imaginations and keep alive the "read to me" spirit. Such books are often those which children might not find for themselves, but can be introduced by an interested adult. These books will arouse curiosity and help children to discover new relationships and gain new insights. They will pose difficult questions, perhaps, and push the listeners into thought-provoking situations. They will feature a wide variety of styles of writing as well as subject matter.

Here is a baker's dozen of books that meet the above criteria. In addition, they are well suited to serialization:

Kelpie, by William Mayne
Hare's Choice, by Dennis Hamley
Catherine Called Birdy, by Karen Cushman
The Ship That Flew, by Hilda Lewis
Flour Babies, by Anne Fine
Mrs. Frisby and the Rats of NIMH, by Robert C. O'Brien
The Forest Family, by Joan Bodger
Abel's Island, by William Steig
Afternoon of the Elves, by Janet Lisle Taylor
Haroun and the Sea of Stories, by Salmon Rushdie
Harris and Me, by Gary Paulson
The Mennyms, by Sylvia Waugh
The Midnight Fox, by Betsy Byars

Don't miss the stories of Australian writer Paul Jennings. Try any of *Undone!*, *Unreal!*, or *Unbelievable*, as well.

Special Read-Aloud Sources

There are many possibilities when choosing books to read aloud, but the following categories offer some additional ways of exploring and finding material. In particular I draw attention to picture books for the older reader, reinterpretation of vintage works, and books that feature the exploration of language.

Picture Books for the Older Reader

Many years ago as a teacher of drama, I was made aware of political and sociological issues, which were being raised in modern picture books. Far from being books that addressed the needs and interests of young children, these books explored territory that was of greater significance to those nine and ten years of age and older.

Children today are powerfully influenced by computers and television. The fleeting nature of so much which passes before their eyes, however, leaves little opportunity for exploration and reflection. The modern picture book represents a significant resource for teachers or parents to use to encourage children to think, discuss, play out, and look again.

Of particular interest to me is the opportunity that these books provide for bringing together children of varying ages and reading ability. The children can take part in shared activity and find a stimulus for further reading and viewing.

In addition to challenging and sophisticated subject matter, the books reflect widely varying styles of expression, providing countless opportunities for comparison and comment. For example, *The Last Giants* by François Place describes a Victorian scientist's discovery of a race of mysterious tattooed giants who sing to the stars and live in harmony with nature and how this discovery leads to their destruction. It is a very moving account of the impact of advanced peoples on primitive peoples. *The Last Giants* could be read alongside Judy Allen's *Tiger* which deals with attitudes and beliefs threatening the existence of this marvellous creature and Anthony Browne's surreal *Bear Goes to Town.* Together these picture books and illustrated stories present a powerful array of perspectives on survival, co-existence, morality, and the consequences of rapid technological change. Much reflection and discussion are made possible.

Here are some other books that illustrate widely varying styles of expression and subject matter:

The Widow's Broom, by Chris Van Allsburg
Ghost Train, by Paul Yee
The Lady of Shalott, by Alfred Lord Tennyson, illustrated by Charles Keeping
Sweet Clara and the Freedom Quilt, by Deborah Hopkinson, paintings by James Ransome
We're All in the Dumps, by Maurice Sendak
Freedom Child of the Sea, by Ricardo Keens-Douglas

The Lotus Seed, by Sherry Garland

The Hockey Sweater, by Roch Carrier, illustrated by Sheldon Cohen

The Dust Bowl, by David Booth, illustrated by Karen Reczuch

Monster Mama, by Liz Rosenberg

Mufaro's Beautiful Daughters, by John Steptoe

The Man Who Wanted to Live Forever, retold by Selina Hastings, illustrated by Reg Cartwright

Anancy and Mr. Dry-Bone, by Fiona French

The Wolf, by Margaret Barbalet

Reinterpretation of Vintage Works

Artists in all fields have proven that reinterpretation of an older work can be extremely innovative. Often an older work possesses a charm or archetypal power, which lends itself to being reworked or translated into contemporary terms. Sometimes, appreciation of the genre, shape or achievements of the original causes writers and artists to want to work within the framework.

In many ways these reinterpretations introduce a new generation to classic stories which they might not otherwise hear about.

Two examples of reinterpretation deserve special mention. Leon Garfield's *King Nimrod's Tower,* which appears in this book, is a superb example of new story which has been invested with the feelings of the original. *Do Not Open* by Brinton Turkle is a brilliant transposition of a story from one historical context (*A Thousand and One Arabian Nights* — "The Fisherman and the Bottle") to another (a twentieth century coastal setting).

Also look for these titles:

Flossie and the Fox, by Patricia McKissack

The Stinky Cheeseman and Other Fairly Stupid Tales, by Jon Scieszka

Snow White in New York, by Fiona French

City of Gold, by Peter Dickinson

The Giant's Toe, by Brock Cole

Does God Have a Big Toe?: Stories about Stories in the Bible, by Marc Gellman

Jim and the Beanstalk, by Raymond Briggs

The Green Children, by Kevin Crossley-Holland

Little Fingerling, by Monica Hughes
The Three Little Wolves and the Big Bad Pig, by Eugene Trivizas

During the past two decades, there has been a vast outpouring of traditional tales resplendent in their new images. The stunning visual treatments given many of these old tales has raised questions about illustrators who are sometimes perceived as indulging themselves at the expense of children's imaginations. While there may be some merit in this argument, there have also been many especially fine retellings featuring illustrations that stretch the viewers' perspective of the story. Here are some outstanding examples:

Hansel and Gretel, by Ian Wallace
Hansel and Gretel, by Anthony Browne
Snow White, by Nancy Ekholm Burkert
The Gingerbread Boy, by Richard Egielski
Rapunzel, by Barbara Rogasky, illustrated by Trina Shart Hyman
The Little Mermaid, by Hans Christian Andersen/Margaret Maloney, illustrated by Laszlo Gal
Snow White, by Josephine Pool, illustrated by Angela Barrett

Books That Feature the Exploration of Language

In addition to already-mentioned books which encourage play with the sounds of language, another source of prolific experimentation is the alphabet. In the dozens of alphabet books that have been published in the last twenty-five years are some of the most innovative adventures with letters one could wish for. I doubt whether teaching the alphabet is nearly so important in these books as engaging the reader in a terrific visual and thought-provoking exercise. Look for the following:

Old Black Fly, by Jim Aylesworth, illustrated by Stephen Gammell
A Prairie Alphabet, by Jo Bannatyne-Cugnet, art by Yvette Moore
The Amazing Hide and Seek Alphabet, by Robert Crowther
A Peaceable Kingdom, by Alice and Martin Provensen
Ape in a Cape, by Fritz Eichenberg
A Calypso Alphabet, by John Agard

Undoubtedly, the most exciting play with language occurs in

poetry. On the whole, poetry receives little attention, yet as a source of delight for children and adults it is unbeatable.

Although offering a wide variety of styles and subject matter is essential, you can't go wrong if you begin with the enjoyment of rhythm. Fun words and fun rhymes powered by pulsating rhythms are a part of playground rituals and games, and in poetry much of the pleasure derives from the mystery of unfamiliar names and strong rhythmic sounds. The verse below appears in *If I Had a Paku* by Charlotte Pomerantz.

Hominy, succotash, raccoon, moose
Succotash, raccoon, moose, papoose
Raccoon, moose, papoose, squash, skunk
Moose, papoose, squash, skunk, chipmunk
Papoose, squash, skunk, chipmunk, muckamuck
Skunk, chipmunk, muckamuck, woodchuck.

Tongue twisters and nonsense verse, riddles and parodies, chants and songs are all good starting points especially because they encourage participation.

The following books are excellent sources for such material:

All Together Now, by Sonja Dunn
Sally Go Round the Sun, edited by Edith Fowke
Mister Magnolia, by Quentin Blake
Alligator Pie, by Dennis Lee
There Were Monkeys in the Kitchen, by Sheree Fitch
The Young Puffin Book of Verse, edited by Barbara Ireson
Don't Eat Spiders, by Robert Heidbreder
17 Kings and 42 Elephants, by Margaret Mahy

Children from eight to ten years of age are often fascinated by story poems that are slightly bizarre and situations that are "off the wall." I think that much of the work of Shel Silverstein, Dennis Lee, Jack Prelutsky, and Michael Rosen appeals for this reason.

Here are some anthologies to consider:

Plum, by Tony Mitton
Songs for My Dog and Other People, by Max Fatchen
Classic Poetry, edited by Michael Rosen

Bad Bad Cats, by Roger McGough
How Do You Wrestle a Goldfish, by Diane Dawber
Another Day on Your Foot and I Would Have Died, poems by John Agard,
    Wendy Cope, Roger McGough, Adrian Mitchell, and Brian Patten
Lizzy's Lion, by Dennis Lee
Rich Lizard and Other Poems, by Deborah Chandra
Till All the Stars Have Fallen, edited by David Booth
Come on into My Tropical Garden, by Grace Nichols

We give a great boost to children's literacy development when we create a nurturing environment where shared experiences with story occur regularly. Under such circumstances, even children who are experiencing difficulty mastering reading skills seem to build and maintain positive attitudes toward stories, books, and reading. These children enjoy stories, relish old favorites, and look forward to new experiences with stories. In short, they acquire a genuine enthusiasm and love for literature.

Fundamentals of Good Read-Alouds

1. Choose a story that greatly appeals to you, pruning it if you see fit.
2. Strive to visualize the story so that you can bring it to life for the listeners.
3. Know your story well. You want to move others, not be taken off guard yourself by hilarious or moving moments.
4. Read slowly, especially at the beginning, to draw in the listeners.
5. Look up from the text regularly and make eye contact with members of the audience.
6. Be attuned to the way the author uses words and say those words clearly.
7. Be playful with your reading, trying different voices for the characters.

SIX

Teaching Students to Retell and Respond to Stories

Brian had not been sitting there long when the old man asked him to tell a fairy tale.

"That is something I never did in all my life," said Brian, "tell a story of any kind."

"Well," said the old woman, said she, "take that bucket and go down to the well below the house and fetch a bucket of water and do something for your keep."

"I'll do anything," said Brian, "except tell a story."

From "The Man Who Had No Story," in *Irish Folk Tales* edited by Henry Glassie

I frequently meet students like Brian who would rather do anything except tell a story. Perhaps they are afraid that they will have to tell a story to the whole class and feel too embarrassed. Perhaps they think that they will have to memorize a story, a task they find daunting. Whatever the reason, it is important to dispel all doubts and fears as quickly as possible. Explain to the students that the purpose of classroom work in storytelling has more to do with developing their versatility as speakers and listeners than it does with performing a story in front of an audience.

Storytelling in the classroom is multi-faceted. It includes elements of listening, responding, retelling, and extending. Our job as teachers is to stimulate the students' desire to engage in these activities.

The best way to learn about stories is to listen to others tell them.

People lucky enough to grow up with an oral tradition often talk about a body of stories which they heard again and again from the lips of a variety of tellers. As one woman in Nova Scotia told me: "When we have a gathering at someone's house we all seem to end up in the kitchen telling stories. Of course we all know the stories, it's how they're told that makes it fun. Nobody tells the same story in quite the same way."

That's the kind of activity and atmosphere I would like to see in the classroom: we can build a body of stories that we all enjoy and discover the many ways that those stories can be told. What we might try to create is a classroom community where everyone feels comfortable making, changing, interpreting, and exploring stories. The emphasis should be on inventiveness and experimentation with the spoken word, I think. Music, visual arts, and drama must also be called into play in order to foster the students' unique interpretations of the tales they investigate.

Responding to Stories Told Aloud

Although listening to and retelling stories is a powerful way to extend the story and language repertoires of students, the relationship between the story and the listener is particularly fertile ground to cultivate. Helping our students express the unique meanings they make as they listen is an important factor in their developing both a strong sense of story and confidence in their own impressions.

I know one young teacher who works very hard to assist his eight- and nine-year-olds to understand how much they can take part in creating the meaning of a story. Once when I was invited to tell a story to his students, I chose a fairytale from Siberia, "The Storm Wife," about three sisters who ventured out in a raging Arctic blizzard to tame a giant, the North Wind. Without such intervention the people of their community would perish. The story is a repeated sequence type in which each sister embarks on the quest and faces certain tasks and tests along the way. Depending on each individual's response to these situations, she succeeds or fails. As is the case in most of these tales, the youngest sibling prevails, the storm is halted, and the people are saved.

For one long minute after I told the story, the students were silent.

Then a voice piped up, "I liked how the story got going and didn't waste time telling you a lot of things."

Another voice cut in, "That story was shaped like a circle."

These voices were quickly joined by others. "I liked how the characters let you know them without a lot of description." "I wonder why the youngest is always the one who is best, most beautiful, and carries off all the honors." "I could see the storm and snow in my mind."

These students knew stories. They also knew how to talk about them without any outside prompting. Their teacher remarked: "I've encouraged my youngsters to pay attention to what has taken place in their heads as they listen and to feel comfortable about speaking their minds and respecting the opinions of others."

Poet Ted Hughes once said that the only interpretations of a story that are of any use are the ones we make for ourselves. "A teacher can help us to our interpretation only by hints and examples that stimulate our self-search. . . ."

Stimulating that self-search was exactly what this young teacher was doing. By encouraging his students to interpret stories each according to his or her own light he was eliciting a wide range of responses which they could think about as they lingered over the story and searched for ideas together. Building on such responses — helping the students to go further than they could go themselves — is an important part of that search.

This is the approach I encourage teachers to take with their students. Let the students go back to the story in a variety of ways. Bring them closer to the story's characters, tensions, and issues. I'm convinced that the memories we take from stories fuel our love of them and serve as important touchstones to literacy. For a story to become memorable, the students *must* have time to revisit it to get to know it and make it their own.

Let's consider some of the ways we might explore the story "Kate Crackernuts," a folktale collected by Joseph Jacobs in *English Fairy Tales*, with our students.

Kate Crackernuts

Once upon a time there was a king and a queen, as in many lands have been. The king had a daughter, Anne, and the queen had one named Kate, but Anne was far bonnier than the queen's daughter, though they loved one another like real sisters. The queen was jealous of the king's daughter being bonnier than her own, and cast about to spoil her beauty. So she took counsel of the henwife, who told her to send the lassie to her next morning fasting.

So next morning early, the queen said to Anne, "Go, my dear, to the henwife in the glen, and ask her for some eggs." So Anne set out, but as she passed through the kitchen she saw a crust, and she took and munched it as she went along.

When she came to the henwife's she asked for eggs, as she had been told to do; the henwife said to her, "Lift the lid off that pot there and see." The lassie did so, but nothing happened. "Go home to your minnie and tell her to keep her larder door better locked," said the henwife. So she went home to the queen and told her what the henwife had said. The queen knew from this that the lassie had had something to eat, so watched the next morning and sent her away fasting, but the princess saw some country-folk picking peas by the roadside, and being very kind she spoke to them and took a handful of the peas, which she ate by the way.

When she came to the henwife's, she said, "Lift the lid off the pot and you'll see." So Anne lifted the lid but nothing happened. Then the henwife was rare angry and said to Anne, "Tell your minnie the pot won't boil if the fire's away." So Anne went home and told the queen.

The third day the queen goes along with the girl herself to the henwife. Now, this time, when Anne lifted the lid off the pot, off falls her own pretty head, and on jumps a sheep's head.

So the queen was now quite satisfied, and went back home.

Her own daughter, Kate, however, took a fine linen cloth and wrapped it round her sister's head and took her by the hand and they both went out to seek their fortune. They went on, and they went on, and they went on, till they came to a castle. Kate knocked at the door and asked for a night's lodging for herself and a sick sister. They went in and found it was a king's castle, who had two sons, and one of them was sickening away to death and no one could find out what ailed him. And the curious thing was that whoever watched him at night was never seen any more. So the king had offered a peck of silver to any one who would stop up with him. Now Katie was a very brave girl, so she offered to sit up with him.

Till midnight all went well. As twelve o'clock rang, however, the sick prince rose, dressed himself, and slipped downstairs. Kate followed, but he didn't seem to notice her. The prince went to the stable, saddled his horse, called his hound, jumped into the saddle, and Kate leapt lightly up behind him. Away rode the prince and Kate through the greenwood, Kate, as they pass, plucking nuts from the trees and filling her apron with them. They rode on and on till they came to a green hill. The prince here drew bridle and spoke, "Open, open, green hill, and let the young prince in with his horse and his hound," and Kate added, "and his lady behind him."

Immediately the green hill opened and they passed in. The prince entered a magnificent hall, brightly lighted up, and many beautiful fairies surrounded the prince and led him off to the dance. Meanwhile, Kate, without being noticed, hid herself behind the door. There she saw the prince dancing, and dancing, and dancing, till he could dance no longer and fell upon a couch. Then the fairies would fan him till he could rise again and go on dancing.

At last the cock crew, and the prince made all haste to get on horseback; Kate jumped up behind, and home they rode. When the morning sun rose they came in and found Kate sitting down by the fire and cracking her nuts. Kate said the prince had a good night; but she would not sit up another night unless she was to get a peck of gold. The second night passed as the first had done. The prince got up at midnight and rode away to the green hill and the fairy ball, and Kate went with him, gathering nuts as they rode through the forest. This time she did not watch the prince, for she knew he would dance, and dance, and dance. But she saw a fairy baby playing with a wand, and overheard one of the fairies say: "Three strokes of that wand would make Kate's sick sister as bonnie as ever she was." So Kate rolled nuts to the fairy baby, and rolled nuts till the baby toddled after the nuts and let fall the wand, and Kate took it up and put it in her apron. And at cockcrow they rode home as before, and the moment Kate got home to her room she rushed and touched Anne three times with the wand, and the nasty sheep's head fell off and she was her own pretty self again. The third night Kate consented to watch, only if she should marry the sick prince. All went on as on the first two nights. This time the fairy baby was playing with a birdie; Kate heard one of the fairies say: "Three bites of that birdie would make the sick prince as well as ever he was." Kate rolled all the nuts she had to the fairy baby till the birdie was dropped, and Kate put it in her apron.

At cockcrow they set off again, but instead of cracking her nuts as she used to do, this time Kate plucked the feathers off and cooked the birdie. Soon there arose a very savoury smell. "Oh!" said the sick prince, "I wish I had a bite of that birdie," so Kate gave him a bite of the birdie, and he rose up on his elbow. By-and-by he cried out again: "Oh, if I had another bite of that birdie!" so Kate gave him another bite, and he sat up on his bed. Then he said again: "Oh! If I but had a third bite of that birdie!" So Kate gave him a third bite, and he rose hale and strong, dressed himself, and sat down by the fire, and when the folk came in next morning they found Kate and the young prince cracking nuts together. Meanwhile his brother had seen Annie and had fallen in love with her, as everybody did who saw her sweet pretty face. So the sick son married the well sister, and the well son married the sick sister, and they all lived happy and died happy, and never drank out of a dry cappy.

At the heart of our work with stories in the classroom is retelling.

Retelling begins when we encourage the students to tell us what they have beheld in their mind's eye. Initially, some students have little to say. I think their concern for finding the right answer gets in the way of their authentic responses. That changes once they know that we are genuinely interested in their personal responses. Some quite good discussion will follow.

Among the most common responses to a story will be the pictures that filled listeners' minds during the telling. As the students describe characters, settings, and incidents that stood out for them, acknowledge the wonderful uniqueness of their interpretations.

Many will mention how they tried to anticipate where the story was heading and how that caused them to think of other stories or personal memories that the story called up.

Questions are a big part of the students' initial responses. Many appreciate that questions they deemed unimportant were on the minds of others too. Especially when we work with traditional stories, students will question values and attitudes which are out of step with the times. Dealing with these issues is extremely important. I don't ever want to ban or suppress stories that may not fit the current framework of political correctness, yet contain elements of truth and beauty which have sustained them over centuries. When these questions arise we can examine, discuss, and if the students desire, remake those parts of the story which do not sit comfortably with them.

Classroom drama affords us an excellent investigative tool for dealing with the controversial parts of stories. We can use drama to get inside the heads of characters and the dilemmas they face. Drama also enables us to build greater contexts around a story and view it from different perspectives. For example, a situation that might be totally inappropriate in our times can take on new meaning when glimpsed from the historical period in which it was set. Simple interviews with story characters can probe the motives for their actions. Retelling the story from a story character's perspective can be quite revealing in terms of tough decisions faced or the unfolding of events. Key moments in a tale can be frozen in time by means of tableaux or examined in detail through movement in slow motion.

Students will also talk about feelings and how they related to experiences story characters were dealing with. Personal memories shared, patterns of story recognized, conventions (such as the Rule of Three) identified, and comments made on how the story was performed are also common responses.

One student reminded me once about how powerfully the storyteller directly influences the responses of the listeners, often unintentionally. I had told a selchie story that day. In the response after the story the student said, "In my mind I saw the selchie maiden as very small . . . not much bigger than a tiny child. But when you came to the part where the fisherman scooped her up in his arms you held your arms out wide and I was startled that she was so big."

Needless to say the student's comment has caused me to exercise more restraint with my gestures as I tell. It has also caused me to value so much the students' retellings of the story they created with me as I told it aloud.

Retelling Stories

Probably one of the best ways to help students make further discoveries about the story is to get it into their mouths. To retell successfully they must rehearse, and the most comfortable way to do that is to have them talk through the story and draw it with a partner. When they work this way, they aren't self-conscious about their explorations. Observe the students constructing narrative and listen to them piece the story together. Doing that will give you a very good idea about how they are using written symbols to represent their knowledge and ideas about the tale.

Sometimes the students make storyboards, sometimes maps, and frequently symbolic representations which capture the tale for them. For example, for "Cap O Rushes," some students drew a broken heart on one half of a page and a whole one on the other half. Around those hearts, they wrote key words to chart story developments. Making drawings always produces better retellings. In all the years I have been working with story retelling and young people, this activity has never failed to prepare students to get the story into their own words and to bolster their confidence.

After twenty minutes or so of graphic depiction it's time to tell the story. (A word of caution: The students will probably want to make pretty pictures and spend precious time coloring in and adding details. Remind them that quick sketches are the order of the day. The aim of the activity is not to make art, but to process our thinking and make a kind of visual script.)

When the students retell, have them sit with their partner so they can see their drawings clearly. Have them decide who will begin and inform the class that you will signal them to switch roles — listener becomes teller; teller becomes listener. The second key to success with story retelling is emphasizing the listener's role as a listener, not as a critic or a blocker. Training the students to play the role of attentive listener is just as important as fostering their abilities as a teller. Until this understanding is well established the quality of the retellings will be somewhat diminished.

Some students will retell so quickly that the story is reduced to information. These students you will need to coach. Encourage them to visualize what their partner is telling them and when they are telling too. Remind them that when they tell a story they have to make everything happen.

If you see that students tend to rush through the story, adopt a drama technique called voice over narration: it will encourage the students to elaborate on their retellings. Have the students work in groups of four. One student retells the story while the other group members enact it in movement or mime as it is told. There is no preplanning; the teller begins and the others must improvise immediately. Once they get the idea of this, the students are quite inventive and in many instances they begin to interact spontaneously, fleshing out the story with movement and gesture and facial expression. From the start make sure the students understand that only the teller uses words. The rest are restricted to movement. This activity serves to free up the story considerably, to increase student confidence, and more importantly, to help them make the story bigger.

The more the students can be taken back to the story, the more discoveries they are able to make. Don't push on if the students have had enough. However, if they are so inclined, here are two additional retelling strategies that you might introduce.

1. Have the students in small groups retell the story from the point of view of a character in the story. (Don't be concerned if they select an inanimate object or a made-up character. I've heard some wonderful retellings of stories done this way.) It's often a good idea to number the students off in their story circles and tell them that whenever their number is called, they take over the telling. This strategy helps the students focus their listening.

2. Invite the students to do a multi-part retelling of the story. This type of retelling resembles readers' theatre without a script. One person in each group takes on the role of third person narrator who will guide and shape the story's direction from its beginning through to its end. Each of the other group members takes the role of a different story character and when called upon will tell the story in the first person through the eyes of their character. The third person narrator begins the story, but often seeks to draw in the point of view of the different story characters. When invited to tell, the characters must advance the story but only from their perspective. The work calls upon the students to improvise within the context of the tale and to listen and concentrate intensely.

Students ten years of age or over are capable of doing a multi-part retelling successfully and enjoy the spontaneity and fun that the activity encourages. For students who want to turn a story into a piece of story theatre, this activity is most satisfying.

When students retell stories in groups in this fashion it is useful to draw attention to how the story has changed from the time they first heard it. I encourage the students to be faithful to the heart of the story (what belongs to the story) but I also want them to understand how their inventiveness can enrich the telling (what belongs to us). Usually the students are quick to point out that expanded dialogue, additional characters, group chants, new information, and changes to the opening and closing are among the innovations they have contributed.

We can also encourage the students to think about how a story might be tuned: when, for example, a slow unwinding style would be most appropriate; with what kind of story a tongue-in-cheek style would enhance the telling; where the sharp staccato rhythm of rap would suit the story.

Throughout this kind of exploration remind the students that they are changing, adapting, and reinterpreting stories just as oral tellers have done since the dawn of human storytelling.

Expanding Students' Vision of a Story

When the students have mastered their retelling of a story we can expand their vision of that tale by plumbing some of the issues and problems with which the characters must grapple. For example, with the story "Kate Crackernuts" the students might do any of the following activities:

(a) Tell them to work in pairs to talk about the images in the story which were most powerful in their minds as they listened, then ask them to draw or paint those images.

(b) Instruct the students to list some of the turning points in the story then conduct an interview with a story character whose thoughts and feelings are revealed at the critical moment. (For example: What was Kate's response when Anne returned with the head of the sheep?)

(c) Students working in small groups could pretend that they learned the story of Kate Crackernuts by hearing it told many times in their family. Each participant could share a two-minute story providing information about the tale that the others don't know.

(d) Have the students build an audiotape bank of stories they can tell. Work in pairs or work in groups, as well as individual tellings, could be placed in the bank.

(e) Ask the students to identify typical ingredients in "Kate Crackernuts" which are common to traditional tales (eg., repetitive plots, fantastical happenings, the Rule of Three). With this in mind have the students research some stories with a partner and prepare to tell one that contains the same features or ones similar to those of "Kate Crackernuts."

(f) Some students might find the double marriage ending to the story of Kate Crackernuts difficult to accept. Have them experiment with other possibilities for reworking the exploits of the heroine.

(g) Ask the students to consider Kate Crackernuts from the standpoint of physical appearance, behavior, and attitudes. In what ways is she typical of story heroines? How is she different? Have the students search for other stories with heroines who either resemble Kate or are quite the opposite. Instruct them to learn their story then retell it in small groups. The group could develop a chart of the stories they heard, highlighting similarities and differences in heroines. (Encourage the students to use examples from a wide variety of cultures.)

One sixth grade class had done an in-depth oral exploration of Antonia Barber's *The Enchanter's Daughter*, a Rapunzel-like story which explores themes of freedom and identity. The heroine must escape her powerful wizard father in order to discover her story. Her escape in the shape of a tiny bird facing impossible odds makes for a gripping tale.

When the oral storytelling exercises had been completed, many students chose to capture some aspect of the tale in writing. For most of these students English was not the first language. Many of them had been in Canada less than six years. Yet the power and beauty of their written expression were quite wonderful. Here are two samples:

Fear and Hope

In such a lonely place
  No one to play with
And no one to talk to. . . .

Little tiny bird
  So small and beautiful
Flying so fast
  Over the mountain

By Handen

Fear and Hope

Lonely as a little lost mouse
Beside the dark old castle.
I stood alone in the moonless night
The wind shook my petal.

My heart pounded faster and faster

BOOM!!!

Lightning struck
Bigger and bigger grew my fear.
I was scared for my life
The rain masked my tears.

Will I ever know
Who was my mother
Or what was my name?

By Irene

When the students have had opportunities to clarify and express their thoughts, to listen to the thinking of their peers, and to enter the landscape of the tale, meeting its characters, exploring their dilemmas, giving voice to their thoughts and possibly restructuring key aspects, they are not only able to retell it to others, but are often eager to express their new ideas or discoveries.

These fresh perspectives might emerge in the form of a new tale arising from the old one, a poem, a painting, a sculpture, a photograph, or a reinterpretation through drama or dance.

If the students want to share the work with others then they have come full circle and the story and its telling live again, not just as a clone of the original but as a product of a stimulated imagination.

SEVEN

Making and Developing Stories in the Classroom

Tommy Trot, a man of law,
Sold his bed and lay upon straw.
Sold the straw and slept on grass,
To buy his wife a looking glass.

— Mother Goose

For the past forty years I have never lost my fascination for nursery rhymes. Above all else I have enjoyed using these powerful elliptical stories with students and extending them into exciting narratives.

As a result, the work of taking a minimal text and building on it I value highly. I think this activity is tremendously important for helping students see the possibilities for taking the germ of an idea and elaborating on it.

Elaborating on Nursery Rhymes

My favorite nursery rhyme has always been "How Many Miles to Babylon?" (This rhyme appears within "Nimrod's Tower" on page 54). I like to say the words and think about the implications of the journey made at night. In drama classes we have built lengthy improvisations and enjoyed reading some of the books that this verse has inspired. I had used this rhyme for many years before I discovered that it could also be played as a game. Here are the instructions for playing it.

How Many Miles to Babylon?

1. Players join hands and form a semi-circle.
2. The two players at the head of the semi-circle form an arch with their arms. Each of these has a name — "black" or "blue" — which is kept a secret from the other players.
3. Players in the semi-circle chant the questions in unison. ("How many miles to Babylon?" etc.)
4. Players forming the arch reply to the questions. ("Three score miles and ten," etc.)
5. When the question/answer chants are finished the players in the semi-circle lift their left foot and chant, "Here's my black." Then they lift their right foot and chant, "Here's my blue. Open the gate and let us through."
6. The players, still holding hands, run through the arch.
7. When the players forming the arch drop their hands, the player caught is asked in a whisper by the gate keepers, "Will you have black or blue?"
8. The captured player, depending on the color chosen, now takes his or her place behind black or blue. As the game proceeds, the gated arch grows larger.
9. When all players have been caught, all the blues and blacks join their arms around the waist of the person ahead, and the blacks and blues face off in a tug of war to determine the game winners.

Equally popular was this nursery rhyme:

The Scrabble Hill Maid

There was a maid on Scrabble Hill
And if not dead, she lives there still.
She grew so tall, she touched the sky
And on the moon, hung clothes to dry.

Students can simply "do" the lines trying out all possibilities for oral interpretation. They can chant in unison as if the verse is a skipping rhyme, divide it into solo and chorus parts, sing it using a familiar tune, or invent some action or movement sequences to suit the words.

Students can also explore between the lines and bring inferential thinking to bear on the text. For example: Who is speaking the words? To whom is the speaker speaking? Why is the speaker saying this? They can brainstorm in groups their ideas about who is speaking to whom and why. Once they have some possibilities it's time to speak the verse out loud to test interpretations. When everyone has worked out an oral interpretation, reconvene and let the groups present their stories.

In the course of one session I heard the lines spoken by a tour guide describing a rock formation used by local residents as a signpost to a mountain pass; children playing a chasing game in the manner of "What time is it Mr. Wolf?"; grandparents relating a ghost story to wide-eyed grandchildren; old folks on a porch reminiscing about childhood experiences; spies sending a code message behind enemy lines; a celestial dreamweaver creating a spell; and the maid herself, returned from the dead to haunt the hill.

Students can go beyond the lines by exploring questions that the story raises. Most groups have little difficulty filling a page. Here is a random sample of the kinds of questions often posed about the maid.

- Were her extreme differences (her size and nocturnal behavior) a cause for personal distress or personal pride?
- Was she the village washerwoman? Did she really hang clothes on the moon? How do you hang clothes on the moon? Could she do it only when there was a crescent moon? Were the phases of the moon actually accomplished by the woman in order to satisfy her drying needs?
- Is this a verse used to describe a pattern of stars near the moon?
- Why was the hill called Scrabble Hill?
- Who might live on a hill with that name? Who left the hill and why? Do folks live there yet? Is there a Scrabble Hill in your community?
- Is this the maid herself talking? Did things ever change for her? Is this her recollection of what others said about her? Is this her form of self-parody? What makes some people the subject of taunting and torment?

To answer the questions the students might conduct interviews in role. Set the scene for them, perhaps in this way:

"You all grew up on Scrabble Hill. Many years ago you left, but today you have returned to visit the place you once knew so well. In a few moments you will return to view familiar sights. As you wander about the hill, survey as many people as you can. Ask them if they remember the 'Scrabble Hill Maid.' Ask them if they know any stories about her."

At the end of the activity, ask everyone to sit down and rewrite the nursery rhyme retaining *only* the original opening line and revealing in the remaining three lines what each understands about the story now they have heard so many tales.

Form a circle and tell the new stories. Through these simple rhymes, hypotheses about that little story are shared and imagined voices added to the story. Furthermore, I am certain that the group will now understand something of the exciting process of building and discovery which storytelling involves.

Here are some new tales that have resulted:

There was a maid on Scrabble Hill
Who frightened every Jack and Jill
Were we so very, very small
That we all thought her 'extra-tall'?

There was a maid on Scrabble Hill
Who choked upon her iron pill
Her neck grew stiff; it would not bend
Her stiff-necked stance lost lots of friends.

There was a maid on Scrabble Hill
She loved to sit beside her still
She drank and drank from her big cup*
And now she cannot give it up.

There was a maid on Scrabble Hill
Who stared at folk and gave them chills
She slept all day and walked the night
And gave us all a terrible fright.

There was a maid on Scrabble Hill
Her love has gone — she waits there still
She hangs out beacons — higher, higher
To lead him home — her heart's desire.

* The cup referred to is supposed to be the Big Dipper.

Between and beyond the lines of such little stories as "The Scrabble Hill Maid" are dozens of stories if we just take the time to think of them. Indeed some of the most poignant storytelling by children, I have heard, has emerged from our attempts to create a set of stories around such little tales.

"Saturday Night" is another wonderful tale to explore.

On Saturday night I lost my wife,
And where do you think I found her?
Up in the moon singing a tune,
With all the stars around her.

Among the stories, inside the story, which children have been quick to identify are these:

(a) attempts to return the woman to earth;
(b) the circumstances that led to the woman's journey into the skies;
(c) the woman's concerns about adapting to a new environment;
(d) the reasons the singing was so important to the adventure.

For each of these stories, the children attempted to identify the storytellers.

For example, in the story of attempts to return the woman to earth, some children decided that the villagers were telling the story. They figured that music was important in the situation and they decided to try to "sing the woman down." Sound poems were created using imaginary moon words and chanted after considerable experimentation with the sound possibilities of the words. When all the poems had been chanted, the villagers were asked to reflect on the event as they recalled it years later and to report what the results had been.

On another occasion, the storytellers were relatives of the woman and the woman herself. In this instance relatives paired off with the woman and attempted to persuade her to return home. They tried to convince her that there were many earthly pleasures she would eventually miss. Those role playing the woman countered with fantastical descriptions of the new life in space.

Other folktales detail similar situations, among them, Alden Nowlan's splendid retelling of the Micmac legend of the Star Brides, which appears below. This story could be studied as an extension of "The Scrabble Hill Maid."

The Star Brides

In the days of the people who are gone two beautiful young sisters were overtaken by night in the woods.

Knowing they could not hope to return to their village before daylight, they made themselves beds of pine boughs and lay down under the open sky, huddling together for warmth.

As they waited for the coming of sleep, they talked, as young girls will, of the young men they might one day marry.

The sky was cloudless and the stars were very bright. Sleep was slow in coming and the sisters were a little afraid. To comfort one another, they pretended the stars were the eyes of lovers, looking down at them protectively.

"I will choose that one to be my husband," said the elder sister, pointing at the sky. "His eyes are as bright as those of a hawk."

"And I will choose that one," said the younger sister, gesturing drowsily, "his eyes are as bright as those of an eagle."

The sisters laughed, fell silent and drifted off to sleep.

Then it was morning. Even before opening her eyes, the elder sister stretched her beautiful arms and legs.

"Be careful!" cried a voice, "you will spill my warpaint!"

Suddenly, the sisters were fully awake. They sat up quickly, their eyes wide with wonderment.

Here were two handsome young warriors. One, with eyes like those of a hawk, leaned on his spear. The other, with eyes like those of an eagle, knelt on the ground to mix his red warpaint.

Perhaps it was in that first instant of awakening that the sisters fell in love. Perhaps it took many days. Perhaps they only imagined that they were in love. In any event, it was not long before they were married: the elder sister to the warrior with the eyes of a hawk; the younger to the warrior with the eyes of an eagle.

For a time, they were happy. While their husbands hunted in the Woods, the sisters cared for their wigwams.

But soon the sisters grew sulky because, near the wigwams, there was a large, flat stone which their husbands had strictly forbidden them to touch or move.

If their interest had not been aroused by their husbands' prohibition, the sisters might never have thought of touching the

114

stone. As it was, they could not rest until their curiosity was satisfied.

So one day when the men were hunting for bear, the sisters pried up the stone and peered under it.

What they saw made them start back and cry out with fear. For the stone was like a trapdoor in the roof of the world.

Far, far below they saw the village of their childhood, surrounded by the forest in which they had fallen asleep.

"Our husbands are not men!" cried the elder sister.

"They are wizards!" cried the younger.

"They are star creatures!"

"And they have taken us to their home above the sky!"

The sisters embraced one another and wept and when their husbands returned home they would not leave off weeping.

"Did you not choose us to be your husbands?" the hawkeyed man demanded.

"Did you not summon us when you lay in the forest?" demanded the eagle-eyed man.

"That was only a game," wept the elder sister.

"All girls play such games," wept the younger.

"Then you wish to return to your world?" asked the hawkeyed man.

"Yes. Oh, yes. Please," the sisters agreed.

"Then you are free to go," said the man with the eyes of an eagle.

"But you must follow our instructions."

That night the sisters were told they must sleep together, and they were to cover their faces.

"In the morning you must not be in haste to uncover your faces," the star men warned. "Wait until you hear a chickadee sing; and even then you must not open your eyes. Wait still longer until you hear the red squirrel sing; and still you must wait. Keep your faces covered and your eyes closed until you hear the striped squirrel sing, then open your eyes and uncover your faces and you will be safe."

The sisters slept little that night and awoke early the following morning. They lay awake for a long time with their faces covered before they heard the singing of the chickadee.

The younger sister wanted to get up at once to see if they had in truth been returned to earth, but the elder sister restrained her.

"We must wait until the singing of the striped squirrel," she reminded. "Be patient. We will soon be back in our own village."

But when the red squirrel sang, the younger sister could control herself no longer. She uncovered her face and opened her eyes. And the moment she opened her eyes she found herself falling through the night — falling faster and faster toward the stony floor of the world.

There was not even time for her to cry out, so her sister did not know she had disappeared until she heard the singing of the striped squirrel, uncovered her face, opened her eyes and found herself in the part of the forest where their adventures had begun.

However, as she looked up at the sky from which she had lately come, the elder sister saw a star falling through the gray of the early morning and knew that star was in fact her younger sister who had uncovered her eyes too soon and was doomed to fall forever toward the earth.

And to this very day when the people see a falling star they say it is the younger sister, still tumbling through the night.

There are even those who say that the morning star is the hole in the sky through which the eagle-eyed warrior observes the eternal descent of his bride.

Here is another nursery rhyme chock-a-block with possibilities for story making.

There are men in the village of Erith
Whom nobody seeth or heareth
And there looms on the marge
Of the river, a barge
That nobody roweth or steereth

I am indebted to Louise Cullen, a program consultant with the former North York Board of Education who wrote the haunting tune that follows. Sing the piece in unison, then try the piece as a two-part round. Work with the sounds of dripping oars and add movements. Perhaps the children could build imaginary barges and row in time to the round. Quite a bit of layering could be tried here.

I have heard wonderful interpretations of the text. Students have pictured the storytellers as sirens haunting the river, weeping women and children awaiting the return of warriors from battle, scolding

There are men in the vill - age of (shh) Er - ith, whom

no - bo - dy see - eth or (shh) hear - eth.   And there

looms on the marge of the   riv- er a barge, that

no - bo - dy row - eth or   (shh) steer - eth.

• Music — Louise Cullen © 1983
• Lyrics — P.D. — The Annotated Mother Goose
Gould & Gould, N.Y., The World Pub. Co., 1967

grandparents using the story as a means of keeping their grandchildren from the water's edge, and prisoners being taken to a dungeon.

One teacher and her class imagined the setting for the verse to be London, England, in the 1800s. They did some research on workhouses, child labor, tenement housing, and conditions for workers in factories, then using role play tried to imagine themselves working on barges on the river Thames. They designed living quarters, tried to figure out sleeping arrangements and meal preparations, then created movement stories of a day in the life of a barge worker.

When the issue of why the barges maintained strict silence and seemed mysterious arose, students decided that the men might be smugglers, thieves, or scavengers. In movement they re-created a typical day in their lives. The teacher, in role as a law enforcement officer, boarded the barges to investigate their activity. The students had to figure out how to avoid arousing any suspicion about their presence on the water.

There are many wonderful collections of nursery rhymes to explore with your students. Raymond Briggs's *The Mother Goose Treasury* is one I like very much. Also look for *An African Mother Goose*, compiled by Virginia Knoll; *Tortillitas para Mama and Other Nursery Rhymes in*

Spanish and English, compiled by Barbara Cooney; and Robert Wyndham's *Chinese Mother Goose Rhymes*.

Many contemporary poets have created works that feature the rhymes, rhythms, and patterns of nursery rhymes. *All Day Saturday* and *Early in the Morning* by Charles Causley, as well as *Jelly Belly* and *The Ice Cream Store* by Dennis Lee, are good examples.

Telling Our Own Stories

The students' own stories and the role these stories play in helping students learn about the world around them, make discoveries about themselves, and explore their own ideas must also shape our work.

A book such as *Tales of a Gambling Grandma* by Dayal Kaur Khalsa can help our students realize how our dreams, our hopes, our beliefs, our memories are shaped and preserved as stories. In this funny and very moving story we learn about a special friendship between a girl and her grandmother.

Often a simple question such as "do you have a special friend?" can trigger dozens of stories. There are other triggers too in the book — family sayings, family treasures, and special places.

Usually, such storytelling is very informal, more like a spontaneous sharing of thoughts, but once the students feel comfortable giving voice to what they are thinking it's very important that the teacher reflect back to them the importance of what they are saying.

Comment positively on both the storytelling and the substance of the story. Sometimes we can draw attention to the way the students so skillfully communicate who what when where as they begin a story. Sometimes we can note a satisfying way that a story has been brought to an end. More often than not a hard decision or a difficult choice is at the core of personal story, and we talk about how that memory, shaped as a story, informs us about who we are.

In the initial stages of this work, students often give elliptical versions of events. To encourage them to elaborate, coach them into re-creating pictures in their minds. A student describing a fall from a bicycle might be prodded gently to picture what was happening before the incident, then during it, and finally after it. Ask if there are any colors, smells, sounds, or feelings that would help us to see the story with greater clarity. There may be a lot of slim anecdotes before students begin to discover what holds the listener.

To help students develop and shape their personal anecdotes it is often useful to have them work in pairs or a group and to direct the listener to ask the teller for more information or details to flesh out the story. Photographs, time lines, and interviews with caregivers will help children to build personal profiles so that they can better think of personal stories. Telling about things that have happened to them involves the students in selecting, structuring, and sequencing.

I have found poetry, especially poems that have as their subject everyday events at home, in school, or in the neighborhood, very effective at prompting personal stories. Here is one by Diane Dawber which has proved to be very helpful in this regard.

How They Do It on TV

Nancy ties me up with a rope we find in the basement.
I'm the good guy — after all, I'm oldest,
She's the bad guy — she's youngest.
We both have on our cowboy outfits —
    vests
    bandannas
    straw hats
    plastic six guns
and we're having fun
chasing one another around the yard
ambushing from the bushes
and yelling "Bang! You're dead!"
We're having fun until
Nancy ties me up
with a rope that we find in the basement.
For someone who's five, she can really tie a knot!
So I can hardly move
and
wriggling to get away
I fall
down the garden steps
knocking all my breath out

forever
I think
the real rope
is no fun in pretend.

When students form their own stories you will probably need to help them slow down the process by considering some of the following:

- Will you tell the story as if it is taking place now or will you tell it as if it happened in the past?
- Will you tell the story in the first person or the third person?

    I have witnessed many examples of students starting a personal story in the third person, perhaps because they are shy of revealing something of themselves, only to slip into the first person halfway through. It bears thinking about this right off the top.
- Do you need to break your story into separate scenes and jot down a few key points for each scene?
- When you try it out with a partner are there changes to be made?

    (I encourage the listening partner to ask questions of the teller about bits they didn't understand.)
- Would you like to tell the story to the whole class or would you be more comfortable in a small group?

Encouraging students to use their own backgrounds as a vehicle for talk and sharing is a natural way to engage them in storytelling. Through this experience they collect their personal stories and develop the skills of asking questions and verbalizing about self and family.

In addition they are provided with an opportunity to display pride in their backgrounds and to discover that some feelings, values, and ideas are universal and timeless. In her book *Black Sheep & Kissing Cousins*, Elizabeth Stone reminds us: "The family's first concern is itself, but its second realm of concern is its relation to the world. Family stories about the world are usually teaching stories, telling members still at home the ways of the world according to the experiences its elders have had."

Family stories such as *Chicken Sunday* by Patricia Polacco, *The Always Prayer Shawl* by Sheldon Oberman, *When the Relatives Came* by Cynthia Rylant, *Tell Me a Story, Mama* by Angela Johnson, and *The Chalk Doll* by Charlotte Pomerantz are excellent models for helping students see these universals.

120

EIGHT

Valuing Children's Own Folk Traditions

Awake, arise, pull out your eyes,
And hear what time of day;
And when you've done, pull out your tongue.
And see what you can say.

— Traditional

Your students possess an oral folk tradition from the street and schoolyard. A simple question such as whether anyone knows a clapping game can become the entry point into a world of riddles, jokes, puns, and other examples of a rich children's culture which exists beyond the school walls. I do meet children from time to time who say they don't know any rhymes, but as soon as you take in a picture book such as *Five Little Monkeys Jumping on the Bed* or an anthology such as *Dr. Knickerbocker* memories begin to click in.

In one schoolyard in Toronto a few years ago, two hundred and fifty children formed a circle and played an elimination game, chanting and clapping loudly as they sought to see who could best avoid having their hands slapped on the count of five.

Stella, ella, olla
Quack, quack, quack, quack
Es chico chico
Chico chico chack chack
Vello! Vello!
Vello vello vellova
One two three four five

It took them fifteen minutes to whittle the circle down to two players and the event was drawn to a close with arm wrestling to declare the winner.

At the school a few blocks away, no one knew this game but the students had some great riddles.

One boy asked me, "What colors do you paint the sun and the wind?" Answer: You paint the sun rose and the wind blue. He said he had made it up. Indeed he might have. I thought it was very clever. His classmates did too.

My point is that our students have a living oral tradition which is a legitimate part of human experience. We should pay attention to this tradition by encouraging our students to collect and share folk poetry. They should gather it in the language of its origin, if possible, illustrate it, and categorize it (e.g., in one school students gathered material under the headings of counting-out rhymes, conversations, stunts, tongue twisters, riddles, stories, games, jokes, and good advice).

All of the material can be recycled too. For example a traditional rhyme can be the source of a new game. It can be elaborated or extended as a larger work or incorporated into a story the student is writing. Note how Grace Nichols and John Agard did this in *No Hickory, No Dickory, No Dock.*

Children's oral tradition is also an important bridge into poetry they will meet in books. The forms, patterns, and wordplay can be linked to what poets do now.

The list on the next page identifies some books that celebrate children's oral folk poetry and play with language.

One area of children's oral folk tradition seems to be disappearing: the singing and drama games. Occasionally I meet some children who can teach me a singing game or a drama game, but it is rare. Fortunately, during my lifetime I have met Bessie Jones, Richard Chase, and Grace Hallworth, and I have learned from them and played the singing and drama games featured here. Probably these are the elements of children's oral folk tradition which you will have to reintroduce or teach your students.

Books That Celebrate Folk Poetry

Picture Books

Each Peach Pear Plum: An "I Spy" Book, by Janet and Allan Ahlberg
Five Little Monkeys Jumping on the Bed, by Eileen Christelow

Anthologies That Feature Children's Folk Poetry

Dr. Knickerbocker and Other Rhymes, by David Booth
Inky Pinky Ponky: Children's Playground Rhymes, collected by Michael
	Rosen and Susanna Steele
I Saw Esau, by Iona Opie

Picture Books That Feature Adult and Children's Folk Poetry

Cat Goes Fiddle-i-fee, by Paul Galdone
A Dark Dark Tale, by Ruth Brown
Hush, Little Baby: A Folk Lullaby, by Aliki
The Tree in the Wood: An Old Nursery Song, by Christopher Manson
We're Going on a Bear Hunt, by Michael Rosen

Anthologies That Feature Adult and Children's Folk Poetry and Stories

And the Green Grass Grew All Around: Folk Poetry from Everyone, by Alvin
	Schwartz
The Singing Sack: 28 Song-Stories from around the World, by Helen East
Walking the Bridge of Your Nose, by Michael Rosen

Anthologies That Feature Traditional Literary Verse

A. Nonny Mouse Writes Again, selected by Jack Prelutsky
Poems of A. Nonny Mouse, selected by Jack Prelutsky
No Hickory, No Dickory, No Dock: A Collection of Caribbean Nursery Rhymes,
	by John Agard and Grace Nichols

Singing Games

Generally, the singing games have only the simplest dance movements: advancing and retreating in lines, circling left or right or winding into the centre, and passing under human arches. Some form of chant or song accompanies the movement; the rest is dramatic action. Spontaneous improvisation is essential to the spirit of the activity.

London Bridge Is Falling Down, Draw a Bucket of Water, and the Farmer in the Dell are examples of well-known singing games.

Perhaps Wind Up the Apple Tree is one of the best of them. Both this and The Allee Allee O! which follows are taken from folklorist Richard Chase's *Singing Games and Playparty Games*.

Wind Up the Apple Tree

A large number of players can be accommodated in this game. The players join hands and form a loose spiral. A player at one end of the spiral is designated Winder. The player at the opposite end is the tree. The players sing in march tempo:

PLAYERS:
Wind up the apple tree!
Hold on tight!
Wind it all day and
wind it all night!

The Winder leads around clockwise while the tree stands still. As soon as any player's arm is stretched out he stops. One by one the players stop and so does the Winder.

PLAYERS:
Stir up the dumplings,
the pot boils over!
Stir up the dumplings,
the pot boils over!

Winder and players terminate the winding up song and sing the jump song. Everyone jumps up and down on both feet as they sing. As this chorus is repeated again and again, the Winder begins to sidestep to the left. The Winder eventually pulls the spiral out straight.

Wind up the apple tree!
Hold on tight! *etc.*

Steady march tempo. Sing it over and over until all are wound up.

Wind up the ap-ple tree! Hold on tight!

Wind it all day and wind it all night!

... a little faster:

Stir up the dump-lings, the pot boils o-ver!

The Allee Allee O!

This game comes from the children of the seacoast town of Rockport, Mass.
(Taken down April 20, 1948)

Oh the big ship's a- sail- ing through the Al- lee Al- lee O, the Al- lee Al- lee O, the Al- lee Al- lee O! Oh the big ship's a- sail- ing through the Al- lee Al- lee O! Hi! Ding- dong- day!

FORMATION

A line of players holding hands. The player on the left end of the line takes hold on a playground post, or leans with the left hand against a tree-trunk or a wall.

STEP

A quiet walk

As the song begins, the one on the right-hand end of the line leads between the tree and the first player, thus winding up number one.

Then

the leader pulls around counter-clockwise and goes between number one and number two, winding up number two, etc. Each turns halfway around when wound up.

Keep on singing and keep on winding them up one by one . . .

. . . until the last one is wound up.

To unwind: Keep on singing, and . . .

the one next to the leader now lifts his left arm and pulls the leader back through.

Then the next pulls both these players through.

The next pulls these three through, etc., until all are unwound. To end, skip in a ring.

126

Drama Games

Drama games form part of the cultural heritage of all people. What children have preserved throughout the ages are the roots of primitive ceremonies of the ancients. The magic in the words, music, and movements is universal and general. It comes from a time when the actions dramatized were the real actions of daily life. The business of love, politics, religion, and warfare were all carried out in the form of social games. Indeed all cultural activities were social games enacted in the play circle.

For a bookless society, social games were the way to remember. Remnants from these times still abound in today's world. Antiphonal singing, impromptu versifying and contests are but a few examples. Iona and Peter Opie point out in *Children's Games in Street and Playground* that "In these games children gain the reassurance that comes with repetition, and the feeling of fellowship that comes from doing the same as everyone else" (p. 2).

Although specific words are given for the games that follow, they represent but one of many variations. In some cases, the words used in the past have been lost; only fragments remain. To these have been added other words from less distant times.

Participants might create other words, lines, or verses, add bold gestures, or create new movements. Such adaptation is the norm for the oral tradition in all times, in all cultures.

Call and response or chiming-in activities permit us to become vocally involved in story. In the following drama games, the feeling of the ancient play circle is re-created as participants join in, not only with voice, but with spontaneous body language.

Johnny Cuckoo

With "Johnny Cuckoo," we leave the circle and the winding and move to a story told in a line. I like to set the scene before entering into this story.

"I want you to imagine that it is the middle of the night and you have been roused from your beds by members of the home guard and herded into the village square. A major battle is in full swing along the front this night and reinforcements are required. A company commander has come to press you into service. As he approaches the villagers break into song. . . ."

GROUP IN UNISON:	Here comes one Johnny Cuckoo Cuckoo, Cuckoo Here comes one Johnny Cuckoo On a cold and stormy night.	—Single player walks toward the line of singers and marches back and forth inspecting the "soldier."
GROUP IN UNISON:	What did you come for, Come for, come for, What did you come for On a cold and stormy night?	
PLAYER:	I come for me (we come for us) a soldier, Soldier, soldier, I come for me (we come for us) a soldier On a cold and stormy night. (slight increase in tempo)	—As Johnny Cuckoo delivers his message, players in the line react in mime.
GROUP IN UNISON:	You look too filthy dirty, Dirty, dirty, You look too filthy dirty On a cold and stormy night.	—Players all turn their backs on Johnny Cuckoo and wiggle their hips at him, turning to face him on the last word.
PLAYER:	I am (we are) just as clean as you are, You are, you are, I am (we are) just as clean as you are, On a cold and stormy night.	—Johnny Cuckoo turns his back on the line and wiggles his hips, turning around and choosing another player on the last word.
GROUP IN UNISON:	Now here comes two Johnny Cuckoos *etc*.	—The game is repeated with two Johnny Cuckoos, at the end of which the original Johnny Cuckoo chooses another player to repeat the game with three and so on.

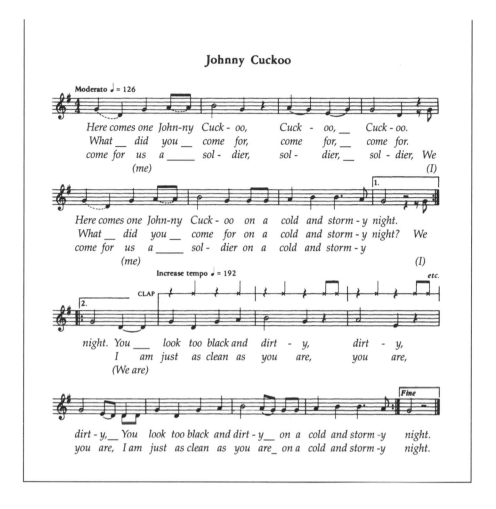

Johnny Cuckoo

Acting and Pretending Games

Closely related to the drama games but perhaps less active are what Iona and Peter Opie have described as acting and pretending games.

In acting games, there is a story, often accompanied by set actions each time the game is played. These games are very old and usually demand that children take on roles which they love, such as ghosts, corpses, and other scary creatures. The example that follows is a traditional English acting game.

Mary Brown

1 CHILDREN: Here we all stand round the ring.
And now we shut poor Mary in.
Rise up, rise up, poor Mary Brown.
And see your mother go through the town.

MARY: I will not stand upon my feet
To see my mother go through the street.

2 CHILDREN: Rise up, rise up, poor Mary Brown.
And see your father go through the town.

MARY: I will not stand upon my feet
To see my father go through the street.

3 CHILDREN: Rise up, rise up, poor Mary Brown.
And see your brother go through the town.
MARY: I will not stand upon my feet
To see my brother go through the street.

Verses about Mary's sister, cousins, uncles, and aunts, and beggars follow.

9 CHILDREN: Rise up, rise up, poor Mary Brown.
And see your sweetheart go through the town.

MARY: I will get up upon my feet
To see my sweetheart go through the street.

(And makes a rush to break the ring that surrounds her.)

From Iona and Peter Opie's *Lore and Language of Schoolchildren* comes this next acting game. A fine story to tell before or after the game is "Tipingee" from *The Magic Orange Tree*, tales from Haiti collected by Diane Wolkstein (see pages 32–35, chapter 2).

Old Man in the Well

Any number of players may join in this game but one must be the mother and one the old man. All the rest are the mother's children. The old man hides himself in a gloomy, mysterious place which is designated as the well. The following dialogue takes place:

CHILDREN TO MOTHER:	Mother, Mother, may we have some bread and butter?	
MOTHER TO CHILDREN:	Let me see your hands. Your hands are very dirty. Go to the well and wash them.	(Children hold out their hands for inspection.)
CHILDREN TO MOTHER:	Mother! Mother! There's an old man in the well!	(The children go to the well where they spy the old man hiding. They rush back to Mother screaming).
MOTHER TO CHILDREN:	Don't be silly, children. There's no one in the well.	
CHILDREN TO MOTHER:	But we saw him!	
MOTHER TO CHILDREN:	It's only your father's underwear. I hung them out to dry. Go again.	
CHILDREN TO MOTHER:	Mother! Mother! There's an old man in the well!	(The children go again, see the old man, and come back screaming.)

The mother tells them again that no one is in the well and makes up another explanation such as "It's only your father's shirt hanging out to dry."

The children are sent back two or three more times until the mother is persuaded to come too. She sends one of the children for a candle (twig), lights it, and accompanies the children to the well.

When they reach the well, the old man blows the candle out, just as she is about to look in.

MOTHER TO NEAREST CHILD:	Why did you blow out my candle?	(She pretends to cuff the child about. Child sets up a howl.)

The mother relights the candle. The old man blows it out.

MOTHER TO ANOTHER CHILD:	Why did you blow out my candle?	(A second child is beaten in a mock fight and howls lustily.)

This action is repeated until every child has had an opportunity for a dramatic howl.

Finally, the old man permits the mother to look into the well. He leaps out screaming and gives chase. The person caught becomes the next old man.

Pretending games, usually less lurid than acting games, deal more with real activities and call for more improvisation. In these games, the players adopt a role within some common situation that they all understand and appreciate. Lemonade is a fine example of a pretending game.

Lemonade

The players divide into two equal teams and stand on parallel goals at least seven metres (or twenty feet) apart. The first team decides on a trade or occupation to be acted out, and then advances toward the other team while the following dialogue takes place.

FIRST TEAM: Here we come.
SECOND TEAM: Where from?
FIRST TEAM: New York.
SECOND TEAM: What's your trade?
FIRST TEAM: Lemonade.
SECOND TEAM: Give us some.

The first team comes as near to the second as they dare and acts out their trade or occupation, each in his or her own way. The second team tries to identify what is being acted out, and when one identifies correctly the first team runs for its goal, while the second team tries to tag them. All who are tagged join the taggers' side. The second team chooses a trade and the dialogue is repeated, followed by the acting, as before. Both sides have the same number of turns, and the one having the largest number of players at the end wins.

Remembering Our Folk Heritage

Whenever these rhymes, games, stories, and songs are played, I am always amazed to see how quickly self-consciousness drops away and is replaced by lively expressions and animated faces. Such moments are very rewarding because they serve to illustrate that our interest and love of the material help us to bring energy to the event.

Even more rewarding is the flood of memories that are released as fragments of verse, expressions, rhymes, and stories come to mind and are spoken. People are often surprised at the extent of their own folk heritage. They are even more surprised that they had never thought to make use of it. How odd it is that we so often forget what we have carried around inside of us all our lives!

I hope that, as a result of exploring their own story words, the students will truly grasp the meaning of I. B. Singer's reminder in *Naftali the Storyteller and His Horse, Sus*:

> When a day passes it is no longer there.
> What remains of it? Nothing more than a story.
> If stories weren't told or books weren't
> written, man would live like beasts — only
> for the day.
> Today, we live, but by tomorrow today
> will be a story.
> The whole world, all human life,
> is one long story.

Professional Resources

Barton, Bob, and David Booth. *Stories in the Classroom: Storytelling, Reading Aloud and Role Playing with Children*. Markham, ON: Pembroke, 1993.

Barton, Bob, and David Booth. *Mother Goose Goes to School*. Markham, ON: Pembroke, 1995.

Blatt, Gloria T. (ed.) *Once Upon a Folktale: Capturing the Folklore Process with Children*. New York: Teachers College Press, 1993.

Booth, David (ed.) *Telling, Retelling and Listening*. Toronto, ON: *Orbit*, Vol. 30 No. 3. OISE/UT, 1999.

Booth, David. *Story Drama: Reading, Writing and Roleplaying across the Curriculum*. Markham, ON: Pembroke, 1994.

Chambers, Aidan. *Tell Me*. Markham, ON: Pembroke; York, ME: Stenhouse, 1996.

Cook, Elizabeth. *The Ordinary and the Fabulous: An Introduction to Myths, Legends and Fairy Tales for Teachers and Storytellers*. Cambridge: Cambridge University Press, 1969.

Dailey, Sheila. *Putting the World in a Nutshell: The Art of the Formula Tale*. New York: H. W. Wilson, 1994.

Fox, Carol. *At the Very Edge of the Forest: The Influence of Literature on Storytelling by Children*. London: Cassel, 1993.

Fulford, Robert. *The Triumph of Narrative: Storytelling in the Age of Mass Culture*. Toronto: Anansi, 1999.

Hamilton, Martha, and Mitch Weiss. *Children Tell Stories: A Teaching Guide*. Katonah, NY: Richard C. Owen, 1990.

Heath, Shirley Brice. *Ways with Words: Language, Life and Work in Communities and Classrooms*. Cambridge: Cambridge University Press, 1983.

Gillard, Marni. *Storyteller, Storyteacher*. York, ME: Stenhouse, 1995.

Jennings, Claire. *Children as Storytellers*. Melbourne: Oxford, 1991.

Livo, Norma J., and Sandra A. Rietz. *Storytelling: Process and Practice*. Littleton, CO: Libraries Unlimited Inc., 1986.

MacDonald, Margaret Read. *The Storyteller's Start-up Book: Finding, Learning, Performing and Using Folktales*. Little Rock, AR: August House, 1993.

Mallan, Kerry. *Children as Storytellers*. Sydney: PETA, 1991.

Miyata, Cathy. *Journey into Storytelling*. Hamilton, ON: Tree House Press, 1995.

Opie, Iona. *The People in the Playground*. Oxford: Oxford University Press, 1994.

Pellowski, Anne. *The World of Storytelling: A Practical Guide to the Origins, Development, and Applications of Storytelling*. Rev. ed. New York: Wilson, 1990.

Pennac, Daniel. *Better Than Life*. Translated by David Homel. Markham, ON: Pembroke Publishers, 1999.

Rosen, Betty. *And None of It Was Nonsense: The Power of Storytelling in School*. Portsmouth, NH: Heinemann, 1988.

Rosen, Harold. *Stories and Meanings*. Sheffield: National Association for the Teaching of English, 1985.

Rosenbluth, Vera. *Keeping Family Stories Alive: A Creative Guide to Taping Your Family Life & Lore*. Vancouver: Hartley & Marks, 1990.

Sawyer, Ruth. *The Way of the Storyteller*. Harmondsworth: Penguin, 1977.

Schimmel, Nancy. *Just Enough to Make a Story*. Berkeley, CA: Sisters' Choice Press, 1992.

Steele, Mary. *Traditional Tales: A Signal Bookguide*. Stroud, GLOS: The Thimble Press, 1989.

Stone, Elizabeth. *Black Sheep & Kissing Cousins: How Our Family Stories Shape Us*. New York: Times Books, 1988.

Stone, Kay. *Burning Brightly: New Light on Old Tales Told Today*. Peterborough, ON: Broadview, 1998.

Swartz, Larry. *Classroom Events through Poetry*. Markham, ON: Pembroke, 1993.

Tatar, Maria. *Off with Their Heads! Fairy Tales and the Culture of Childhood*. Princeton: Princeton University Press, 1992.

The National Storytelling Association. *Tales as Tools: The Power of Story in the Classroom*. Jonesborough, TN: National Storytelling Press, 1994.

Yolen, Jane. *Touch Magic: Fantasy, Faerie and Folklore in the Literature of Childhood*. New York: Philomel, 1981.

Zipes, Jack. *Creative Storytelling: Building Community, Changing Lives*. New York: Routledge, 1995.

For more information on storytelling, contact

The Storytellers School of Toronto
791 St. Clair Avenue West
Toronto, Ontario
M6C 1B7

National Storytelling Association
P.O. Box 309
Jonesborough, TN USA
37659

nsn@naxs.net

Index of Tales and Verse

(First lines of verses appear in roman type.)

Index

Acknowledgments

My thanks to the following individuals:
David Booth, who has contributed to my work in so many ways for more than forty years,
Diane Dawber and Lissa Paul, who always find answers to my difficult questions,
Joan Bodger, Diane Wolkstein, and Dan Yashinsky, who helped me get started on this journey,
Kaye Lindauer, who has shared our storytelling sessions at the statue of Hans Christian Andersen in Central Park for nearly a quarter of a century,
Judy and Hy Sarick and the staff of the former Children's Book Store for helping me find great stories,
Myra Barrs, Cathy Miyata, Bill Moore, Brenda Parres, Lynda Pogue, Marion Seary, and Larry Swartz for their endless enthusiam and support,
my publisher, Mary Macchiusi, and editor, Kate Revington, for their meticulous care and interest in this project,
and last but not least, Doreen Barton, whose behind-the-scenes toil made everything possible.

Credits

Every effort has been made to acknowledge all sources of material used in this book. The publishers would appreciate it if any errors or omissions were pointed out, so that they may be corrected.

Acknowledgment is gratefully made for the use of the following copyright material:

"The Bamboo Tower" by Jan Knappert in *Myths and Legends of the Congo*. Copyright Jan Knappert.

"Crystal Rooster" from *Italian Folktales*, selected and retold by Italo Calvino, translated by George Martin, copyright 1965 by Giulio Einaudi editore, s. p. a. English Translation copyright 1980 by Harcourt Brace Jovanavich, Inc.

"Hominy, succotash, raccoon, moose" from *If I Had a Paka*, by Charlotte Pomerantz, copyright 1982

"How They Do It on TV" from *How Do You Wrestle a Goldfish*, by Diane Dawber. Copyright Diane Dawber, 1997. By permission of Borealis Press Ltd.

"I'm Tipingee, She's Tipingee, We're Tipingee, Too" from *The Magic Orange Tree and Other Haitian Folktales*. Collected by Diane Wolkstein. Copyright ©1978 by Diane Wolkstein. Reprinted by permission of the author.

King Nimrod's Tower by Leon Garfield and Michael Bragg. Copyright ©1982 by Leon Garfield.

"Mary Brown" from I. & P. Opie's *The Singing Game*, copyright Oxford University Press 1985

"The Old Man in the Well" from I. & P. Opie's *Children's Games in Street and Playground*, copyright Oxford University Press 1969

"The Star Brides" by Alden Nowlan in *Nine Micmac Legends*. By permission of Nimbus Publishing, Halifax, Nova Scotia.

Excerpt from "One" from *When I Dance* by James Berry. Copyright 1988 by James Berry. Reprinted by permission of the author.

"Wind Up the Apple Tree" and "The Allee Allee O!" by Richard Chase in *Singing Games and Playparty Games*, by permission of Dover Publications, New York

"Fear and Hope" by Handen and by Irene, reprinted by permission of Anne Kong